SpringerBriefs in Ethics

For further volumes:
http://www.springer.com/series/10184

Lisa Newton

Ethical Decision Making:
Introduction to Cases
and Concepts in Ethics

 Springer

Lisa Newton
Shelburne, VT
USA

ISSN 2211-8101   ISSN 2211-811X   (electronic)
ISBN 978-3-319-00166-1   ISBN 978-3-319-00167-8   (eBook)
DOI 10.1007/978-3-319-00167-8
Springer Cham Heidelberg New York Dordrecht London

Library of Congress Control Number: 2013934534

Printed on acid-free paper

Springer is part of Springer Science+Business Media (www.springer.com)

Contents

1 **Cases and Decisions** 1
  1.1 The Impaired Driver 1
  1.2 Definitions and Distinctions 3
  1.3 Definitions of the Terms of Ethics 6
    1.3.1 ADAPT: An Approach to Moral Decision-Making 7
    1.3.2 ORDER: Confronting Complexity 9
    1.3.3 DEAL: Carrying on Without Resolution 14

2 **The Principles of Ethics** 23
  2.1 Beneficence: People are Embodied 24
  2.2 Justice: People are Social 25
  2.3 Respect for Personal Autonomy: People are Rational 26
  2.4 The Human Condition 27
  2.5 The Basic Imperatives 28
  2.6 Some Cases to Illustrate the Dilemmas 31
    2.6.1 End of Year Bonus 31
    2.6.2 Baby Samantha 32
    2.6.3 The Alcoholic in the Workplace 33

3 **Professional Ethics** 39
  3.1 What Constitutes a "Profession"? 39
  3.2 Professional Ethics and Market Ethics 41
  3.3 Professionals in Business 42

4 **Some Considerations from Moral Psychology** 45
  4.1 Evolutionary Psychology: What Darwin Tells Us About
    How We Think 45
  4.2 Acquiring Morals: The Track of Education 50
  4.3 Failing to Acquire Morals: What Can Go Wrong 56
  4.4 The Work of the Moral Psychologists: The Trolley Dilemma 57
  4.5 Conclusion 61

Bibliography 63

Chapter 1
Cases and Decisions

How do we make ethical decisions, decisions that will stand up to challenges?
Consider the following case.

1.1 The Impaired Driver

You have stayed about an hour longer than you intended to at a very pleasant party with your old college friends. While you were getting your law degree and starting practice, your roommate Marty made it big on Wall Street. He hosted the party in his huge Riverside Drive apartment. All the old college ties were there—great memories, beer, booze, marijuana… hadn't seen *that* in awhile. Good stuff, too.

Realizing you're late, you race to the parking garage, elevator to the third floor, hop in your SUV, and tear around the turn toward the exit. Smash! Car parked in just the wrong place. You hit it dead center. You back up, get out, note that there is extensive damage to the other car—both doors on the driver's side badly dented—but none to yours. What should you do?

You know damn well what to do. There's clearly damage, lots of it, so you have to take out your cell phone, call the police, and wait there till they come. Watching you propping yourself up against your SUV, they'll insist on the inconvenience of a breathalyzer test. When they get the results of that, they'll give you a chauffeured ride to the precinct station and insist further on a urine test. When they get the results of that, you may get to know the folks in the precinct very well before you see the sky again. You may very well—probably will—lose your license to operate a motor vehicle. The fines will be substantial; you may lose your SUV. You may even go to jail. The damage to your reputation, and to your position in your law practice, will probably be irreparable; depending on the state, they may yank your license to practice law. That's a lot to think about. Meanwhile, you are the only occupant of this parking garage at this hour. You could just drive back to Connecticut and not say anything to anyone.

What to do, indeed. The standard ethicist's injunction, "Do the right thing," may entail a terrible cost, and it is the agent, not the ethicist, who has to absorb it. Let's think about it.

L. Newton, *Ethical Decision Making: Introduction to Cases and Concepts in Ethics*,
SpringerBriefs in Ethics, DOI: 10.1007/978-3-319-00167-8_1, © The Author(s) 2013

How do we make decisions in these cases? This is as good a place as any to introduce some of the terminology we'll be using more systematically in the parts that follow.

1. What course of action will cause the greatest good to the greatest number, minimizing pain to all parties and maximizing happiness? We call this kind of thinking **consequentialist**, or **teleological** (from the Greek word for "end" or "goal"), since it judges the moral quality of the action by its consequences or by the end it achieves. In classic **Utilitarianism**, as set forth by **Bentham** (1823) and **Mill** (1863) the only consequences that matter are **happiness and unhappiness**, pleasure and pain, for everyone affected by the act. Measuring pleasure and pain for all parties, including your family, the owner of the other car, even the world at large, it looks like your best course is to take off for Connecticut without doing anything at all. Drive slowly so you don't get stopped. After all, the pain felt by the car owner upon finding his damaged car is nothing compared to the pain that you and your family would feel if you lost your ability to earn a living, let alone if you went to jail. Besides, his insurance will probably cover the whole bill.

2. Yes, but think of it this way. That law is there for a purpose. What you are supposed to do, as a citizen, right now, is call the police. That's your **duty.** You've enjoyed all the benefits of citizenship, now it's time to honor your part of the bargain. **What if everyone who got into an accident just took off? Would the world be a better place?** Could you approve of a law that said, when you find you've caused damage to life or limb or property, if it isn't convenient to stay around, just take off? If you can't, and you probably can't, then you have no right to make an exception of yourself in this case. That rule is the substance of **Immanuel Kant's Categorical Imperative**, which he set forth in his Groundwork of the Metaphysics of Morals (1785): Act so that you can simultaneously will that the maxim of your action (the reasoning that led you to do it) should become universal law. In heading back to Connecticut without calling the police, you set yourself above the law and contribute to a lawless society. Kantian reasoning is called **non-consequentialist**, or **deontological** (from the Greek word for "duty"), since it looks not at the consequences of the action but at the law or duty that governs it.

3. Here's another way to think about what you're doing, or about to do. When you get home, suppose you find your father, or the rector of your church, or your older brother, or anyone you trust, love, and admire, sitting in the kitchen. Somehow he knows what happened in that garage, and he asks you to explain just what you did, confronted with that difficult situation, and your reasoning to your decision. **Why did you do what you did?** Well, how would you explain it? How would you justify taking off like that, when you were clearly in the wrong? If that scenario doesn't suggest an approach to the problem, put a reporter from *The New York Times* (or *The Wall Street Journal,* if you're that type) sitting beside him in another kitchen chair. The reporter is going to describe the whole situation, including your reasons for acting as you did, **in**

the newspaper tomorrow, on the front page. What kind of person would you look like in that story? Is that the kind of person you want to be? There are certain traits that we value in ourselves and others, traits like honesty, integrity, and courage, that we call **virtues**. Morality is not just about consequences, nor is it just about laws and duties—often it's about the sort of person you are, your very being, so we call the reasoning that draws on these considerations **virtue-based** or **ontological**, from the Greek word for "being." **Aristotle** (4th century BC) based his Ethics upon ontological reasoning; we've never really lost track of it.

These are agonizing decisions, and they govern life—the future life of the person who has to make them, and the way history will judge her or him. More complex decisions are addressed in the discipline of ethics, and the rest of this chapter will consider more complicated dilemmas; but we must not forget that the fundamental moral quantities are honesty, integrity, and courage, those that the impaired driver must call upon right at the moment he finds himself alone in that garage with a smashed car in front of him.

1.2 Definitions and Distinctions

One thing we know for sure about ethics, is that it concerns matters in conflict, dilemmas, matters that people get upset about and argue about. What matters might those be? Socrates (469–399 BC) took on this problem exactly, according to Plato. He and a friend, Euthyphro, have agreed that the gods often disagree with each other, and indeed, that there are regular wars in heaven. Now, Socrates wonders, what might cause the gods to get into violent quarrels? and he suggests the following distinctions:

> *Socrates:* What sort of disagreement is it, my good friend, that causes enmity and anger? Let us look at it in this way. If you and I disagreed about the question, which of two numbers was the greater, would this disagreement make us hostile and angry with each other? Shouldn't we quickly settle a dispute of this kind by having recourse to arithmetic?
>
> *Euthyphro:* Certainly.
> *Socrates:* And suppose we disagreed about the relative size of two objects, shouldn't we quickly put an end to our quarrel by having recourse to measurement?
> *Euthyphro:* Quite so.
> *Socrates:* And I presume that we should settle a question of relative weight by having recourse to weighing?
> *Euthyphro:* Of course.
> *Socrates:* Then what would be the subject of dispute about which we should be unable to reach agreement, so that we became hostile to one another and lost our tempers? Very likely you can't say offhand; but consider, as I suggest them, whether the required subjects are questions of right and wrong, honor and dishonor, good and bad. Isn't it when we disagree about these, and can't reach a satisfactory decision about them, that we become hostile to one another... you and I and all the rest of mankind? (Plato, *Euthyphro,* 7A–7E).

We still use these distinctions, in just this form, but they've acquired new names. There turn out to be three kinds of sentences, distinguished (just as Socrates pointed out) by the way we **verify** them, i.e., the way we find out **whether they are true**.

1. **Logical, or formal, statements** are definitions or statements derivable from definitions, including the entirety of mathematical discourse (e.g., "$2 + 2 = 4$," or "A square has four equal sides"). Such statements can be **verified by a formal procedure** ("recourse to arithmetic") derived from the same definitions that control the rest of the terms of the field in question (i.e., the same axioms define "2," "4," and the procedure of "addition"; the four equal sides and right angles define the "square"). True formal statements are **analytic: they are true logically, necessarily, or by the definitions of the terms**. False statements in this category are **self–contradictory**. (If you say, "$2 + 2 = 5$," or start talking about "round squares," you contradict yourself, for you assert that which cannot possibly be so—you conjoin ideas that are incompatible). A logically true or logically valid statement can never be false, or disproved by any discovery of facts; it will never be the case that some particular pairs of 2 do not add up to 4, or some particular squares turn out to be circular—and if you think you've found such a case, you're wrong! "$2 + 2 = 4$" is true, and squares are equilateral rectangles, as philosophers like to say, **in all possible worlds**. For this reason we say that these statements are **"true a priori"**: we can know them to be correct prior to any examination of the facts of the world, without having to count up lots of pairs of pairs, just to make sure that $2 + 2$ really equals 4.

2. **Factual, or empirical, statements** are assertions about the world out there, the physical environment of our existence, including the entirety of scientific discourse, from theoretical physics to sociology. Such statements are **verifiable by controlled observation** ("recourse to measurement," "recourse to weighing") of that world, by experiment or just by careful looking, listening, touching, smelling, or tasting. This is the world of our senses, the world of space, objects, time and causation. These empirical statements are called **synthetic,** for they "put together" in a new combination two ideas that do not initially include or entail each other. As a result they cannot be known a priori, but can be determined only **a posteriori, that is, after investigation of the world**. When they are true, they are **true only contingently, or dependently, as opposed to necessarily;** their truth is contingent upon, or depends on, the situation in which they are uttered. (As I write this, the statement "it is raining out" is true, and has been all day. The weatherman tells me that tomorrow that statement will be false. The statement "$2 + 2 = 4$," like the rectangularity of squares, does not flick in and out of truth like that).

3. **Normative statements are assertions about what is right, what is good, or what should be done.** We know these statements as **value judgments,** prescriptions and proscriptions, commands and exhortations to do or forbear. **There is no easy way of assigning truth value to these statements. The criteria of "truth" that apply to formal and factual statements do not apply**

to normative statements. This is why, when we disagree about them, we become "hostile," and "lose our temper" at each other; there is no easy way to resolve the dispute. We can certainly say of such judgments (formally) that they conform or fail to conform with other moral judgments, or with more general and widely accepted moral principles. We can also say (empirically) that they receive or fail to receive our assent as a society, as compatible or incompatible with our basic intuitions of what is just or right (as determined by a poll or survey). We may also say that a judgment succeeds or fails as a policy recommendation on some accepted pattern of moral reasoning, like adducing consequences of that judgment and estimating how human wants will be affected should it become law (see the section on Moral Reasoning, below). But the certainties of math and science are forever beyond the grasp of any normative system, which is, possibly, as it should be.

One limit on normative reasoning is important enough to get clear at the outset. You can't get an "ought" from an "is"; you cannot derive any normative statement from any collection of facts, no matter how emotionally compelling, without a previously accepted normative statement as premise. From the fact that a certain product line is unprofitable, it does not follow automatically that the company should abandon it; from the fact that the new medical technology can prolong the patient's life for another 6 months, it does not follow automatically that the patient should elect to use it; from the fact, verifiable by poll, that the nation overwhelmingly does not want to pay any more taxes, or approves of abortion, it does not follow that taxes are wrong or abortion is right. Other things being equal, we may very easily accede to the "ought" premise—that a company should do whatever will improve the bottom line, that medical science ought to prolong human life, that in a democracy, what the people prefer is or ought to be, law. But cases test these rules all the time, and we want to be free to examine them when the situation seems not to fit the intent of the rule. At these times **we must be very clear on what is factual— verifiable by survey, experiment, or observation—and what is normative.**

These distinctions, universally valid, are part of every introduction to philosophy. But why are they necessary to understand ethics? The most important reason to be familiar with these distinctions is that occasionally disputes that seem to be about values or moral principles are actually about facts or about the meanings of words. Such disputes are resolvable, at least in principle, and they should be disposed of before the discussion continues.

For as Thomas Hobbes pointed out, words have no value in themselves. They are but tokens, and wise men do but reckon with them (for fools, they are money). There is **no point in arguing about the meaning of a word**. Simply define your terms to begin with, doing your best to place your definition within range of the normal discourse of the field, and carry on your discussion from there. Only one thing is essential: that you know when a dispute is about the meanings of words and when it is about something more important, and that you agree at the outset that whatever you decide to let the words mean, you will not let that agreement influence the final decision.

How will we use the terms of moral discourse? Any text on ethical theory has to open with the observation that of all matters in ethics, the meanings of the terms has caused the most acrimony and dispute. Since the earliest of the Socratic Dialogues, we have argued about the meaning of key terms like "morals," "ethics," "virtue," "piety," "justice" and the others, all the others. Given the limited purposes of this text, I will simply stipulate at this point how I intend to use the key terms of ethics, observing only that my usage is not bizarre. More than that will no philosopher claim.

1.3 Definitions of the Terms of Ethics

In what follows you may expect the following words to be used in general in these ways:

Morals or Morality: the **Rules** and *prima facie* **Duties** that govern our behavior as persons to persons. All you really need to know you probably learned in kindergarten. The rules and duties are easy to know and to remember—but very hard to follow consistently.

Examples:
   Don't hurt people (As your kindergarten teacher would have put it, Don't hit.)
   Be nice, create happiness (Help the teacher, be kind to the little kids).
   Be fair, practice justice (Share your toys, don't take the biggest piece of cake).
   Respect the rights of others, honor their choices (Keep your hands to yourself!)
   She would probably have added others:
   Always tell the truth.
   Be clean and neat, Take care of your health.
   But essentially, the first four will do as a basis for morality.

Values: States of affairs that are desired by and for people and that we want to increase; also called ends, or goals.
Examples:
   Health (as opposed to sickness).
   Wealth (as opposed to poverty).
   Happiness in general.
   Freedom, Justice, Democracy, Rule of Law.

Virtues: Conditions of people which are desirable both for the people themselves and for the good functioning of the society.
Examples:
   Wisdom (vs. ignorance, irrationality).
   Courage (vs. weakness, unreliability).
   Self–control (vs. greed, violence, indulgence).
   Justice (vs. egoism, favoritism, deviousness).

Ethics: Properly speaking, the academic study of morals, duties, values, and virtues, to find their theoretical links and relationships, and how they work together (or do not) in practice.
   Other understandings of the term **ethics:**
   1. More generally, the whole field of morals, moral rules, duties, values and virtues—the whole study of our attempts to order human conduct toward the right and the good.

2. More specifically, a **professional ethic** is a particular code of rules and understandings worked out by the members of a profession to govern their own practice. (See Appendix on the Professions, below).

Ethical Principles: Very general concepts that sum up a range of morals, values and virtues, from which moral imperatives can be derived. We test our actions against **Rules,** our rules against **Principles.**

Sometimes Ethical Reasoning is helped by a decision procedure, or template, suggesting a pattern of steps to follow in order to solve puzzling problems. Here are three that we have found useful.

1.3.1 ADAPT: An Approach to Moral Decision-Making

People naturally want to do good and avoid evil. For the most part, we limit our attention to morality to the observance of certain interpersonal rules—of courtesy, helpfulness, and respect for privacy, for instance—that serve to make daily life more livable. But sometimes a condition comes to light that interrupts, imposes itself upon, daily life. Consider the following case:

Hurricane Katrina has devastated New Orleans. Following the hurricane, which in itself did not do as much damage as some had feared, the levees that protect the city broke, and the city was immediately flooded. Many families, especially in Ward Nine and others of the poorer districts, were stranded by the flood and in terrible danger—from drowning, from disease (there was no potable water), from hunger, from lack of access to health care, and eventually, from roving gangs. Somehow, they had to be gotten out of there.

Why hadn't they left earlier? As the hurricane closed in on the city, the mayor had ordered a general (voluntary) evacuation, either to areas outside the city or as a last resort to the Superdome. Experienced residents sized up the relative dangers of hunkering (or sheltering) in place, risking severe winds, or of being evacuated by school bus to unprepared areas outside of town, to a mobbed Superdome, or to some distant city, while their property stood empty and unprotected. Many stayed.

Then the flooding started, and the mayor had ordered a general evacuation. All the usual means of transportation were useless. Only boats could be used for evacuation, so the National Guard was put into boats to bring the people out. The entire nation was watching, angry that the residents had not been brought out earlier; there was a lot of pressure to get the job done.

Then the difficulties began. Some residents willingly climbed into the boats with a small well-organized pack of personal goods. Others would not leave without their pets. Some of these were coerced into the boats and wept miserably the entire trip. Some had aged spouses or parents who were too sick to move. Some pointed out that the gangs would ravage their houses if they left, and refused to leave. What were the Guardsmen to do? Herd them in at gunpoint? Respect their free choice and leave them in the flood, perhaps to die?

Eventually more facts came to light: the Superdome had turned into a living hell when it lost electricity and water; the places out of town were sometimes no more than camping places under bridges, in the broiling heat of summer; the distant cities were less than welcoming to second and third waves of refugees. Meanwhile, as municipal, state and federal governments feuded over who bore the ultimate responsibility for the mess, Ward Nine was abandoned to its fate; it will probably never be completely rebuilt.

The Katrina case, as we may call the situation, exhibits certain characteristics that plague the moral life of the nation.

First: some condition is brought to light, some situation, or array of facts. This condition captures our **attention**, alerts us to something that stands out from the background noise of our lives as requiring our concern.

Second: that condition is discussed, the information is disseminated through the community, a community **dialogue** is conducted where public opinion is actually formed. That "community," incidentally, may be as small as a family or as large, as in this case, as the whole nation.

Third, the discussion incorporates the moral **assumptions** that guide our lives, ordinarily without conscious thinking about. We do not have to reason out what we ought to do in most situations; most of the moral work is already done. Lives have to be saved; that is not in question.

Fourth, **proposals** for action are put forward and policies adopted. Decisions are made, implementing the imperatives in a way appropriate to the situation that caught our attention.

And Fifth, the results of the action are **tested** against the results expected. The test results are fed back into the data from the initial situation: Was the action taken in fact appropriate? Were the imperatives successfully implemented? Or should we go back to the drawing board, and introduce new proposals for action or policy? The decision process, on review, does not return to the starting point, but only asks after the effectiveness of the policy for action—we have agreed about the ends of the proposed action, and now we seek the most effective means.

From the above, we can put together a normal moral reasoning procedure, easily remembered in the acronym ADAPT:

Attention
Dialogue
Assumptions
Proposals
Test.

(Note: allow me to apologize right now, for this and subsequent acronymic tricks of this sort. They give the appearance of slickness, I know, but they really do help us to remember.) These normal procedures are used whenever changes in our world require new policies in order to continue normal life in accordance with our ordinary commitments.

Now consider the following cases:

(A) You are a physician called into confer with the family of a terminally ill man in a nursing home. He is conscious, in some discomfort, confused much of the time. He will not get much better, but his heart is strong, and he is not expected to die soon. His children (his wife is dead) are distressed at the length of time it will take him to die. They would like you to inject a fatal dose of morphine to hasten death, on grounds that his estate is being eaten up by the medical and nursing home costs.

(B) You are the production manager of a pharmaceutical company under a lot of competitive pressure. Your boss suggests that you could double productivity if you filled half the penicillin ampules with saline solution instead of penicillin. To be sure, the patients wouldn't get the penicillin prescribed, but most penicillin prescriptions are unnecessary anyway, so probably it wouldn't do anyone any harm.

In practice, cases A and B would probably not call forth any high-level moral reasoning. They are for you, we may suppose, new cases; but the Assumptions that have always worked for you will work here. Physicians do not kill their patients; children do not kill their parents to accelerate the inheritance; you do not deliberately adulterate product runs or market trash under a product's label. The answer is No; if asked for reasons, the normal **ADAPT**–level reasons will do. Try, for instance, "That simply is not done." Or, "That's just not acceptable." More personally, you might say, "I couldn't sleep nights," or, "I couldn't look at myself in the mirror when I shave tomorrow, if I did anything like that." More spiritually, you might try "My religion forbids me even to consider anything like that," or more ominously, "I don't look good in an orange jump suit." The moral rules that back these up are clear to all: practice medicine only for the benefit of the patient; never tell lies, especially to customers.

Principles and reasoning based on consensus morality are not always in such good shape. Recall the Third Reich (1930–1945), and the fact that in Germany in Hitler's time, it was accepted practice, and in accord with the religious intuitions of the leaders of the country, and definitely in accordance with law, to kill Jews wherever you found them (in an orderly manner, of course). **That is why we have to know ethics; to know when the principles and reasoning that we ordinarily use need to be re-examined, criticized, and maybe changed—to know, in short, when ADAPT is not sufficient.**

1.3.2 ORDER: Confronting Complexity

A problem of moral concern, rules or character—like the impaired driver's desire not to confront the cops, the heirs' desire to dispatch their rich father, the boss's desire to make a quick profit, or the distress of the poorer residents of New Orleans—is not the same as an ethical dilemma. In a moral problem, we know what is right, but we may have very good reasons not to want to do it, or we may be puzzled about the right way to say "No" or the best means to obtain the best outcome. (Additionally, we may be tempted to preserve our level of comfort by doing nothing at all!) In an ethical dilemma, we really do not know the right thing to do. Consider the following case:

> Peter and Dora Vlasovic, 51 years and 43 years of age respectively, are at a loss as to what to do about Dora's 67–year old mother, who lives with them. She is suffering from Alzheimer's disease, and while her periods of confusion are not yet continual, she is becoming too unreliable to be left alone. Both husband and wife work outside the house, and cannot stay with Mother during the day. They started looking into appropriate Nursing Homes, but Mother, who was a schoolteacher and fiercely independent all her life, has put her foot down: no Homes. "Look, you know how valuable my mind and my dignity have been to me," she finally said to them. "I simply cannot endure the thought of ending my days tied in a chair drooling on my lap. See that pillow on my bed? When I can't function any more, my life is over, as far as I'm concerned, and I want you just to put that pillow over my face and sit on it for about 20 minutes. Just call the doctor in the morning and say I died in my sleep. I won't contradict you. No Homes."

Meanwhile, the couple has found out that the cost of these Homes is well beyond their means, and that Mother will be left on Medicaid after her assets are gone. Their own assets are not large, and they would be totally responsible for the costs if they hired nurses to come to the house to take care of her. They also have teen-age children, approaching college, to think about, who will need money for college and probably financial help as young adults after their education is finished.

"How did people used to handle this type of situation? Before there were Nursing Homes?" Dora had once asked her doctor. "Easy," he had replied, "People didn't used to live this long. And when they did, in this state, with no other choice in the matter, people simply left them home alone, tied down or roaming wherever they wanted to roam." That did sound "easy" to Dora, but on balance, worse than the other alternatives. They have the house to think of, too, and leaving Mother alone all day sounds like playing Russian Roulette with house and Mother both.

But their first concern is for Mother. The life projected for her does not really seem to be worth living, the more they think about it. "Putting a pillow over her face" is a dreadful thought, of course, but it is what Mother wants, and if they can't face the pillow, the Hemlock Society advertises many more humane ways to bring life to an end. Should they go the pillow route? Should they explore the "rational suicide" alternatives with Mother? Or should they insist on the Home (or put her there anyway after she is no longer organized enough to resist)? Or should they devastate their own financial resources with hired nurses? Are there other alternatives?

In our attempts to reach the good or just solution in this case, what approach do we take? Typically, if we are (personally) in the middle of cases like this, we are strongly tempted to grasp at whatever "solution" appeals to us at the moment: that is, whatever solution accords with our previous prejudices and tendencies. But one of the major objectives of the teaching of ethics is to draw us beyond that subjective stance to one where all rational persons could agree that the right course, or *a* right course, is being pursued. That means that we must reach a course of action that is objectively right, or at least open for public scrutiny.

What would constitute an orderly approach to such problems? First, as participants and decision makers, we should

organize our options in the situation—what alternatives are really open to us? and note the probable outcomes of each. What, in this situation, is it possible, and reasonable, for us to do? And what will be the likely results of each of those choices? Which of the outcomes on the list are totally unacceptable? They should be eliminated, and the rest left for further consideration at a later stage. In this step, we are reasoning *teleologically* or *consequentially,* looking to the means that will produce the most desirable ends.

The Vlasovics, in this case, have the options of

1. Leaving Mother alone—and risking her and the house. That's not acceptable, save for very short periods of time.
2. Bringing in nurses by the day. That will turn out to be very expensive.
3. One of them quitting whatever else they're doing and just taking care of Mother. That will lower the family income, for all purposes, substantially, and no one wants either the burdensome task or the loss of income.
4. Putting that pillow over her face. The thought makes everyone queasy, and they really don't want to go to jail.
5. Putting Mother in a home. She will complain, but she will be safe, and the rest of the family can continue their own lives. This may also be very expensive, until they can establish Mother's eligibility for Medicaid.

Before they act, however, they must

review the rights of the various participants, for legally protected rights, in our system, trump, or override, considerations of right outcome. We must also respect moral (usually legally enforced) **rules** that are held to be valid regardless of the consequences. That is an important point: in this step we are reasoning *deontologically* or *non-consequentially*; that which violates a rule is prohibited by that rule no matter what consequences flow from doing or omitting the act.

Two of the most powerful rights and rules confront us in this situation:

First, the *right of the individual to refuse* the well-meaning ministrations, for his or her health and safety, imposed by others without consent. Mother does not want to go into a Home, and that should settle that. Medicaid has nothing to do with it.

Second, the option preferred by Mother herself, the pillow placed over her face, violates a stringent *rule against voluntary homicide*, "thou shalt do no murder." It is not our purpose at this point to enter the emotional debate about the permissibility of assisted suicide or euthanasia, as requested by a competent patient. At the time that the pillow route would have to be followed, Mother would not be competent to request anything of the sort, and placing pillows over faces does not qualify as physician-assisted euthanasia. The act would be homicide, in fact murder in the first degree, and there are very good reasons why our society forbids it. If Pete and Dora take this option, they will have violated that rule.

Meanwhile, there are other rights to be taken into account. The minor children have an absolute right to their parents' support, for maintenance (food and shelter), affection (yes, that's a right), and provision of education. To what extent will care for Mother have an impact on them?

When we have our options clear and our rights and rules factored in, we should

determine our decision, make a **disposition** of the problem, for the moment. The situation will not wait, after all; an initial decision must be taken immediately. For the moment, Mother is rational, and peaceable, enough to be kept at home with her family; also, during her periods of lucidity, she enjoys being with them and they enjoy her. Perhaps a local daycare program can take her during school hours, and the teenagers can switch off afternoons to be with her before Pete and Dora come home from work. Nurses can be hired in occasionally to give everyone a break. The solution can't last forever; will it work at all? Note that the family *must* act, with very incomplete information. That imperative is typical of such dilemmas. Pete and Dora decide to try it. And then, in a few days, weeks, or months, they must

evaluate the effects of the decision. The decision and the action do not, as Macbeth pointed out, trammel up the consequences. The world continues. We need to follow up, to find out what results our decisions have had. The Vlasovics, in this situation, will not be able to avoid the results; Mother is still in the house with them. How much are the teenagers losing from their sacrifice of their afternoons? The answer to that will depend very much on the peculiarities of this family's situation. How is Mother responding to the new program? That depends very much on the peculiarities of Mother. The trouble with ethical dilemmas, as opposed to ethics as a discipline, is that the real solution is empirical, day to day, trial and error. Finally, we have to

review the situation, reconsider the decision, with an eye toward *revision*. Nothing, in human affairs, is ever set in stone. We make our decisions, usually, for today, knowing that the decision will probably produce a new situation, with its own new dilemmas, and we will have to take on the whole problem again. The Vlasovics' decision to keep Mother home without round-the-clock nurses, bringing her to day care as often as they can, has saved them money, but after awhile it will not work any more: most day care programs cut off when the disease renders the patient violent or incontinent, and new arrangements will have to be made. But by then, there will be a new situation, with a different set of options, and possibly, a revised set of rights. The children, for instance, will eventually leave home, and confront their parents with a completely different set of demands. The federal government, for another instance, changes its mind every month about what programs to fund for the elderly; these will have to be taken into account in future deliberations.

This decision procedure, like many others in the field of ethics, covers all necessary bases for rational decisions. I prefer it to the others only because it builds in, as others do not, the recognition that nothing is ever decided–not well, anyway–once for all. The temptation to come to resolution, to solve something forever, is enormous. Resist it. Situations change, and the more flexible our decision procedure, the better suited it is to the messy world of human conduct.

Like ADAPT, this decision procedure for ethical dilemmas can be remembered easily by its acronym, ORDER:

O: options and outcomes
R: rights and rules
D: determination, decision
E: evaluation of effects
R: review, reconsideration

While we're at getting down procedures that are easy to remember, we may take note of three preliminary steps that have to be taken before we can put things in ORDER:

First, we have to **define the dilemma** that we are facing. What conflicts make the situation difficult to deal with?

> In the Vlasovics' case, the dilemma is painfully evident: how to ensure Mother's and the family's *welfare* while respecting Mother's *choices* and the most serious *rules* of our society, while allocating the family's not-abundant resources *justly* among the generations that call upon them.

Second, we have to conduct empirical **inquiries** as appropriate, discover the facts, get as much **information** as we can.

> What day-care programs are available? What about support groups, for patients and caregivers alike, at the local hospital? Can we get her church involved? How fast is Mother's disease progressing? What should we know about advance directives, living wills, therapies? Our options, once the decision procedure is engaged, will depend upon what is available.

Third, we have to **sort out the stakeholders**. We mentioned above that it is important to know whose interests are to be taken into account in making any decision.

> Part of the work of sorting out the stakeholders is to make sure that all whose interests are really affected are taken into account. Another part of the work is to see that *non*–stakeholders who seek to attach themselves to a decision—the nosy neighbors, for instance, who don't like the cars of the visiting nurses parked (legally) on the street—are excluded from influence on the decision. Of course, that means that we may not take *their* happiness—the satisfaction they derive from running other peoples' lives—into account.

The rights of the family take precedence over the preferences of their neighbors: *rights trump likes and dislikes*. This is why mere appeals to the "greatest happiness of the greatest number" are not always sufficient to decide ethical dilemmas. On the same principle, more commonly, we do not allow neighborhoods to exclude persons of an ethnic background different from that of the current residents, even though it would make all the neighbors overwhelmingly happy to be able to do that. The right of the minority family to live where they choose trumps the preferences of the neighbors not to let minorities live there. Of course the neighbors *are* stakeholders to some extent—they certainly have a right to be protected from Mother's wandering, should it come to that. The Anglo-Saxon Common Law, of which we are the inheritors, has spent patient centuries working out the details of the rights that people have vis-a-vis the neighbors, and we must be conscious of the whole corpus of that tradition.

So our first three determinations, in any ethical decision process, are of the definition, the factual information, and the stakeholders. If it makes it any easier to remember, think of these steps as a "DIS" preface to the "ORDER" decision procedure:

D: Definition of the Dilemma
I: Inquiry to obtain all necessary Information
S: Sorting out the Stakeholders

This leaves us with a procedure whose steps are easy to remember, but leaves the field of ethics in **DISORDER**! Insofar as this DISORDERed formula helps us to remember the essential messiness and anguish of ethical dilemmas, that serves our purposes very well.

Let's revisit cases A and B in the last section, and add some complications:

Case A, but Dad is unconscious, and expected to remain so. He apparently has no sense or feeling, is unable to think or communicate. He may be in some pain sometimes, however, and the children, backed up by the court-appointed conservator, request that he be put on a morphine drip "to make sure he doesn't suffer at all."

Case B, but your boss suggests only that you speed up the process from penicillin culture to filling the ampules, raising a 2 % probability that the drug dispensed will not be up to strength. That doesn't sound good; but there is no evidence that such a change will hurt anyone at all. Meanwhile, the extra income generated will pay off some serious short term debt and put the company in a better position to carry on its research. The quality control manager, who would prohibit this change on general principles, has just retired, and the company is "searching" for another, so you have a probable three–week window during which you can get the new standard drug on the market.

In these cases, the need for higher level reasoning is evident. Terminally ill patients should certainly be kept comfortable; there is nothing to be gained from prolonging this man's life, but a heavy dose of morphine? A balancing act begins, weighing the legitimate, if distasteful, interests of the heirs against the duties associated with the practice of medicine, especially the duty to protect one's patients, especially against this sort of proposal. Ultimately the principle that prevails will be an intermediate one, grounded in the practice of the profession: drugs are there to heal, not to kill, and the patient, probably unable to feel anything and certainly defenseless, may not be subjected to the needs and desires of others.

In case B, the harm caused by the acceleration of the manufacturing process is not at all certain—even if penicillin was never prescribed unless it was needed, the mix of batches would ensure that no patient actually got perceptibly less than the proper dose. Here too an appeal to a middle level principle is necessary. The manager must ask himself, not, what are the consequences of this action? but, what would happen if everyone did this? what would be the general consequences of a rule that permitted or required this action? (That formulation of a middle level principle is found, by the way, in the major works on ethics of Immanuel Kant, John Stuart Mill and John Rawls; see the case of the Impaired Driver, above, and the reference section at the end.) The "Golden Rule," Do Unto Others As You Would Have Them Do Unto You, is a similar principle. Research is important, and debt-retiring is surely good, but for now they may have to wait for alternative sources of funding.

1.3.3 DEAL: Carrying on Without Resolution

We may note that we have been presupposing throughout that the parties to the dilemmas were all in agreement on what the problem was and that it must be solved. In the messy real world of human life, these presuppositions do not always hold. Sometimes problems are particularly resistant to solution, because the interests or moral or religious commitments of the stakeholders are resolutely opposed, because the parties simply cannot understand each other, or for some other reason. Consider the following case:

1.3.3.1 The Abortion Clinic

Michael and Maureen O'Connell are college educated young professionals. Mike is a physician with a practice in Brooklyn and Maureen teaches in the nearby elementary school. They live with their five children (ages 4–13) on the quiet block in Queens where Maureen was brought up, just two blocks from St. Luke's Roman Catholic Church, which they all attend. They are staunch Catholics, as is most of the neighborhood, and they uphold all the public teachings of the Church—including the prohibition of the use of contraceptives, the strict rules regarding any sexual relationship outside of marriage, and of course the absolute prohibition of induced abortion.

The neighborhood is mixed residential and commercial, so they are not surprised to find that a storefront three doors from their house is being renovated for use by a new tenant. "Surprise" does not describe their reaction, however, when finally the medical equipment is moved in and the sign is hung in the window: "Pregnancy Termination: Clean, Quiet, and Confidential." They're living virtually next door to an abortion clinic!

The neighbors want the clinic out: they all, men, women, and children, picket, obstruct patients and their companions, shout "Abortion is Murder!" sing hymns, pray loudly, threaten individual doctors and nurses, court the press, and plan a lawsuit. The clinic operators, on the other hand, led by two gynecologists, Dr. Alan Bennett and Dr. Rita Holmes, want the clinic to stay where it is and run successfully. They know that there is a good market for this service, they know that the women, pregnant against their will, will often resort to coat hangers and back alley butchers to get abortions, if safe abortions are not available legally, and they know they have the law on their side. They too spend time explaining their side to the media, and they demand better police protection.

The neighbors bring the lawsuit. It loses. The clinic is entirely within its rights. The police are ordered to protect the clinic and its workers from violence, a job that they detest: many of them are from the Queens neighborhoods that produced Mike and Maureen, and attend St. Luke's or some church of similar persuasions.

At this point the mayor becomes involved. The common wisdom has it that the elected officials lose three ways in these conflicts. First, they lose the votes of that and all similar neighborhoods, for "allowing the murder of infants a few yards from where our children play." Second, they lose the votes of liberals for not putting a more forceful stop to the demonstrations. Third, they lose the respect of the police department and those interested in law enforcement for diverting resources away from drugs and violent crime. Meanwhile the controversy itself, playing out through the newspapers, presents a very unfavorable view of the present administration. So the mayor wants peace among the parties, peace so quiet that the subject will disappear from the papers, but more importantly, since this is an ongoing issue, peace that will last. How can he, and the city, obtain this peace?

First, can he persuade the neighbors that the business will do them no harm, or the clinic managers to quietly move their clinic elsewhere? We do not usually honor neighborhood objections to a new business in their backyards; as above, not many neighborhood preferences are given enough weight to override the individual's strong interest and prima facie right to live where he wants and work wherever the zoning laws will permit his business establishment. The neighbors should be used to that. But there may be many, and trivial, reasons for locating a business one place rather than another. Maybe the clinic won't mind moving; his office could help with the moving expenses. Like any good politician, his first thought is to make a DEAL.

The mayor chooses Mike and Maureen, as knowledgeable citizens and leaders of the demonstrations, and the physicians, Alan and Rita, as principals in the clinic, to engage in discussions of the issue. There are two reasons for this move. First, they may be able to come to some accommodation that will satisfy both sides permanently (that would have been the purpose of discussion in the last section). But the politician also knows that dialogue is good for its own sake: as Winston Churchill put it, "as long as you 'jaw, jaw' you can't 'war, war.'" In the process of talking, the parties become less hostile and hateful with each other.

No significant accommodation or compromise will work, as it turns out. It doesn't take the mayor long to learn

1. that Mike and Maureen and all their neighbors strongly believe that the human life of a baby begins at conception, that their belief is informed by medical and scientific knowledge (regarding the implantation of the genetic code, for instance) and firmly and rationally held, and that consequently, and quite logically, they really feel that each and every induced abortion is the murder of an infant. They feel that they are living next door to a Nazi Death camp, and that they are bound by religious and moral obligations to speak up and protest the slaughter. They are especially horrified at the prospect of raising their children with this clinic next door, having to tell them what it is about, effectually rubbing their noses not only in state-approved slaughter but in the daily consequences of promiscuous sexual activity!

2. that for their part, Alan and Rita of the physicians' group, the Women's Health Cooperative, that bought the building and set up the clinic, know very well what they are doing and plan to do. They are very much aware of the sexual behavior (if not the sexual ideals) of Mike and Maureen's neighborhood. One half of their first two months' practice were young, unmarried, white, terrified, Roman Catholic girls, mostly from the neighborhood. They feel very strongly not only that they are providing a desired service, but also that they are saving the futures of these girls, permitting them to finish their education, sparing their parents the shame, and the taxpayers the expense, of dealing with the illegitimate offspring, and most likely saving the child from abuse. In the remainder of their practice, mostly older working women of all ethnic backgrounds, they see themselves as permitting adults to carry on their work lives, plan their families and ensure proper provision and education for their children. In both cases, they are an available alternative to the astronomical rates of the offshore clinics, the back alley incompetents and the terribly dangerous self-induced abortion. Their rates are low; they are not in this for the money, but for the public service, and they belong right where they are.

When pushed to the wall, the mayor notices, the two sides argue very differently, apparently reflecting a difference in the way they see the world. Mike and Maureen cite moral rules and rights—the Natural Law, the Ten Commandments, the Right to Life, which hold regardless of situation or consequence. In short, they are reasoning **deontologically** or non-consequentially. Alan and Rita, on the other hand, call attention to the pain felt by the women contemplating unwanted pregnancy, the negative effects on employment, education and general life prospects of the woman, from bearing unwanted children, and the welfare costs and other negative outcomes from denying abortions. In short, they are reasoning **teleologically** or consequentially. While there are also deontological pro-choice arguments and teleological pro-life arguments, **in general Alan and Rita are focused on the problems they are solving, while Mike and Maureen are focused on the nature of the act itself,** and there is not likely to be any resolution between the two sides.

So the mayor proposes an experiment in peacemaking. One of the features of the clinic that troubles the neighborhood most is the mingling of the clinic patients and the children as they depart for or return from school. Could the clinic open at 9:30, a bit later than the morning rush, and take a late lunch break at 2:45, as the children return? In return, the demonstrators will not picket weekdays between opening and that break.

That concession—given that each side views the other's work as fundamentally criminal—is strictly speaking unethical for both sides: any concession is incompatible with the moral beliefs that they have set forth and clearly defended.

After a week or so the mayor's office does an assessment of how the experiment is working. The neighborhood seems quieter, and the newspapers have backed off. Good.

So two of his best mediators bring the four principals back together to attempt further progress. Will the clinic accede to even shorter hours in return for complete removal of the pickets? A few more grudging concessions are obtained; since the prospects for further progress are not good, and the situation seems stable as it is, the mediators back away and let the two parties live with the agreements reached so far.

By continuing the dialogue, even more than joining it to begin with–when each party could have claimed a genuine hope of converting the other–the two sides have acknowledged each other's legitimacy. While there is no possibility of coming to agree with the other's moral stand, there is no hope of destroying the other. Neither one is going away. Distasteful as it is, each must live with the other in peace, even while retaining the conviction that what the other is doing is fundamentally wrong, immoral. This stage of the moral life, a necessity only in pluralistic societies like our own, could be called, possibly, live and let live, or leave people alone!

Change in the neighborhood, or the practice, could upset the unhappy peace that has descended; others must be prepared to step in, should violence break out again, to restart the dialogue. For **DEAL**, the peace process that we have just set forth:

Dialogue
Experiment
Assessment
Legitimacy

is, like ORDER above, fundamentally an iterative process, continually restarting in slightly different conditions.

Let's conclude the cases we started above:

Case A, with Dad unconscious as before, not expected to wake in this life, but occasionally in some discomfort. But this time the children (two of them, twins) do not agree as to what to do about him. One of the twins wants everything done, including surgery if necessary, to "save Daddy's life," and threatens to sue if treatment is "negligently" withheld. The other wants that morphine drip to "ease the pain" and incidentally to shorten Dad's life, and has brought in a lawyer to argue against any "futile" interventions. No document signals which of the twins is to have the power to decide.

Case B, modified as above, but the pressures are worse: the company will have to close the plant, ending 10,000 jobs, and the region's only source of antibiotics, unless productivity takes a marked turn for the better in the next quarter. It is possible that the weakened antibiotic could cause some harm, at least in some extended sickness, but it is not likely to cause death. On the other hand, it is entirely predictable that if the layoff takes place, dysfunction, sickness and death—divorce, alcoholism, mental illness, diffuse chronic illnesses, suicide—will claim a solid percentage of those unemployed 10,000. An undetermined number of patients might suffer if they cannot get their antibiotics on time. The solution to the manager's dilemma is not immediately clear, and intermediate principles do not really solve the problem (**for a thought experiment, try applying the Golden Rule to the case, letting first the workers and then the customers fill the role of "others"**). Here the balance must be struck between the obligations to shareholders, workers, local community, and others with a stake in the continuation of the business enterprise, and obligations to customers, reputation, society at large, and others with a stake in the integrity of the procedures of that enterprise. (For instance, the public surely must be notified about the change in standard—but how?) The principles of concern for the welfare of those affected by a decision—primarily the employees, in this case—and of justice, in following the rules applicable to all no matter what the consequences, are logically independent, and there is no safe formula for deciding which shall take priority in a given case.

Given the nature of the situations to which it is applied, DEAL does not really yield a conclusion that we can all accept as "ethical." (For another real-life application of this "unethical" reasoning, try the dispute between Israelis and the Palestinian Arabs.) But DEAL has much to recommend it, from the ethical point of view. Without further elaboration at this point, we can point out that it accomplishes three tasks, all of which are required by general ethical imperatives.

1. **It promotes the maximum social welfare obtainable**, by preserving the peace and preventing violence. Whatever may divide the physicians, the anti-abortion activists, and the uninvolved neighbors—and there is much that divides them—they share a common interest in the preservation of life, limb, and property, and the grudging accommodation reached serves to protect those shared interests.
2. **It enforces justice, by promoting an even-handed compromise**. Both sides find the state of peace with the other, especially with regard to the concessions they had to make to obtain it, really repugnant. But the fact that they both had to make concessions, and that they are required to stick to the deal they made, makes it fair, even though the fairness may be much more evident to a dispassionate outsider than it is to the parties.
3. **It insists on the dignity, worth, and conscience of every individual**, worthy of respect even from those who are utterly convinced he or she is wrong. Neither group has the right to destroy the other, to keep it from the public space or public attention, to relegate it to a slavish state or second-class citizenship. It affirms, therefore, freedom of conscience, and the right and duty of every human being to develop and inform that conscience, to discern, articulate, and defend a moral position on serious matters, especially matters of life and death.

Those are not small accomplishments. Nor are those principles arbitrary. But in this world where evil cannot always be redeemed, we must keep open the possibility that there may be conditions so evil that the principles must be set aside to confront the evil. Presumably, the Death Camps in the Third Reich presented such conditions. Fortunately for the human race, it is difficult to think of others.

Appendix: The Moral Commitments of Ethics and Subjective Relativism as a Continuing Temptation

Morality, the domain of the fixed rules that govern conduct, is a precondition for ethics, in two ways. First, morality, as a shorthand way of referring to all our transactions with each other, is the subject matter of ethics, just as our transactions with the physical world form the subject matter of science. Second, **ethics is an activity, and any activity requires certain moral commitments of those who take part in it.** We cannot do anything well without moral commitments to excellence, or anything for any length of time without the moral virtue of perseverance. The doing of ethics also has moral commitments appropriate to it. **These commitments, to reason and to impartiality, or to the moral point of view, can rightly be demanded of any person who would take ethics seriously.**

In any troubling case, we have first of all **an obligation to think about it**, to examine all the options available to us. We must not simply act on prejudice, or impulsively, just because we have the power to do so. We call this obligation the **commitment to reason**. The commitment to reason entails a willingness to subject one's moral judgments to critical scrutiny oneself, and to submit them for public scrutiny by others; further, to change those judgments, and modify the commitments that led to them, if they turn out (upon reflection) not to be the best available. This commitment rules out several approaches to moral decision-making, including several versions of

intuitionism (a refusal to engage in reasoning about moral judgment at all, on grounds that apprehension of moral truth is a simple perception, not open to critical analysis), and all varieties of
dogmatism (an insistence that all moral disagreements are resolved by some preferred set of rules or doctrines; that inside that set there is nothing that can be questioned, and that outside that set there is nothing of any moral worth).

Second, we have an obligation to **examine the options from an objective standpoint,** a standpoint that everyone could adopt, without partiality. We want to take everyone who has a stake in the outcome ("stakeholders," we will call them) into account. Since this consideration for other persons is the foundation of morality, we call this perspective **impartiality**, or as Kurt Baier called it in a book of that name, **the moral point of view**. The commitment to the moral point of view entails a willingness to give equal consideration to the rights, interests, and choices of all parties to the situation in question. This commitment to impartial judgment has one essential role in the study of ethics: once we have decided that all persons are to count equally in the calculations, that each is to count as one and as no more than one, we have the unit we need to evaluate the expected benefit and harm to come from the choices before us, to weigh the burdens placed and the rights honored. We also know that if anyone's wants, needs, votes or choices are to be taken seriously and weighed in the final balance, then everyone's wants etc. of that type must be weighed in equally; that is, **if anyone is to be accorded respect and moral consideration, then all must be**. We can derive most of the moral imperatives that we will be using from this single commitment.

By way of example, the familiar Golden Rule, that we ought to treat others as we would have them treat us, is a fine preliminary statement of those commitments. With regard to anything we plan to do that will affect others, we ought not just to go ahead without reflection; we ought to ask, how would we like it if someone did this to us? That consideration is perfectly adequate as a satisfaction of the moral commitments that precede ethics. *In general it may be said, that if we will not agree to submit our decisions to reason, and to attempt to see the situation from the point of view of all who are caught up in it, it will be impossible for us to do ethics.*

Subjective Relativism as a Challenge to Ethics

A superficially popular approach to ethics in America today is known as subjective relativism; as it happens, it violates both of those commitments, and has the effect of making ethics impossible. To make the commitments clearer, it may be worthwhile examining the errors of this simple dogma.

Relativism denotes any approach to ethics which holds that there are no absolute or unchanging moral principles, but that the rules that govern each situation are to be determined by their relation to something else: the customs or culture of the country, for instance, or the desires of the participants. Subjectivism insists that the sole source of knowledge or authority is in the perception of the individual. Subjective relativism, then, as a philosophical position, declares that each person is his own authority on the moral life, and source of his own moral principles at any given time (there is no obligation to stick with principles you may have adopted at another time) and that there simply is no external truth or standard by which that individual authority might be evaluated. On this reasoning, each person not only has the right to decide at any time on all matters of right and wrong, but any decision he or she makes is right, or at least as right as any other. According to subjective relativism, what's right for you may not be right for me (and vice versa), because no one has any right to "impose morality" on anyone else. So there is really no point to arguing about decisions on matters of morals, or learning all about "justifying" moral judgments according to "reason," because there is no need to justify them any way at all. And that is why, subjective relativism concludes, there is no need to study ethics. Note that the position is both anti–reason (there is no need, or way, to subject moral judgment to reasonable criticism) and dogmatic (on the areas of morality that affect me, my opinions constitute an absolute and final authority, not to be questioned by others.) We will get nowhere with ethics as long as this view is taken seriously. But it *is* taken seriously, in that world that lies outside our classrooms, and it is instructive to see why.

The usual justification of subjective relativism seems to follow this line of reasoning. First, we live under Constitutional government—protected by a firm Bill of Rights. Freedom of Speech is the name of one of our fundamental beliefs. Freedom of Speech entails freedom of conscience: each person has the right, indeed the obligation, to think out ethical and political issues and to come to reasoned conclusions on ethical and political matters. Further, each person has the right (within certain obvious limits) to express that opinion without anyone else having the right to object to, or anyway interfere with, such speech. Further, we live in a pluralistic democracy. We are a collection of very different cultures, but we are agreed on two basic principles: first, the innate dignity of each individual, and second, the right of each cultural community to maintain its identity, including its characteristic beliefs and teachings (as long as these are within the law). That means that we have a duty to treat all citizens with respect; we also have the duty to promote tolerance, or, a better word, acceptance, of all our citizens, for what they are and for the culture from which they come.

Meanwhile, we consider it very bad manners to go around telling people that we think they are wrong, especially morally wrong. But if we have many different cultures, we are bound to have disagreements, including serious disagreements, about matters of morality.

All these points add up to respectful disagreement. In America, it is one of our proudest boasts that *any two citizens can very seriously disagree with each other on matters of policy and moral right, and yet each will treat the other with respect, and no instrument or agent of the state will attempt to suppress either of them.* So far, so good.

But it is psychologically a very short step, and a very wrong step, from respectful disagreement to indifferentism or subjective relativism. We make a very large mistake when we confuse a constitutionally guaranteed right with the moral category of rightness. There is no logical connection between what you have a right to do, and the right thing to do; but there is a psychological temptation to move from one to the other. Let's say that again: In logic, there is no connection between "You have the right to think what you like" and "Anything you happen to like to think is right." You have the right, after all, to contradict yourself; you have all the right in the world to think that "2 + 2 = 5." That doesn't make it correct. But psychologically, **once you have told me that no one has the right to correct me when I claim certain sorts of opinions, you certainly seem to have told me that any such opinions are right, or at least as right as opinions can be.**

In mathematics, of course, there is one right answer. In ethics there may not be, since ethical concepts are logically independent, and the question of what weight to assign to them must often be decided on the configurations of a particular case. That is why there can be honest, and possibly irreconcilable, disagreement on matters of ethics. But there are always better and worse answers, answers more or less in conformity with those concepts. There are real moral values. Several of these real values, by the way, are evident in the argument in defense of subjective relativism, given above: the integrity of the human conscience, the sanctity of individual rights, the autonomy and dignity of the human person, the appreciation of cultural variety, and general good manners.

Subjective relativism is not self–contradictory as a position: it makes perfectly good sense to posit the individual as a moral authority in his own case in all instances. But the thesis is self–annihilating, for two reasons. First, it is impossible to defend it without ceasing to be a relativist (since it requires a defender to argue from a basis of absolute values like democracy and freedom). Second, it is impossible to maintain a consistently subjective relativist position without admitting the legitimacy of the attempts to impose moral beliefs—especially successful attempts by the powerful to impose moral beliefs on the powerless—that the proponents of subjective relativism aimed particularly to oppose.

Think of it this way.

Suppose I claim to be a subjective relativist, with every right to have my own opinion respected as true, or at least as true as any other, on all matters of morality. Now, should you challenge me to defend subjective relativism, I would find that probably the only way (and certainly the most persuasive way) to do it would be to appeal to the right of every individual to freedom of thought. I might say, "Each person has a right to reflect on moral matters and reach his or her own conclusions," or, "Human dignity requires respect for individual moral conclusions," summed up as "No one has any right to impose his or her values on me." Now, as it happens, respect for the individual and for individual liberty, along with cultural diversity, are values that you (as a non-relativist) are probably perfectly content to accept as almost absolute and certainly permanent. Suppose you point that out to me, and ask me, having used such values from the outset, if I am now willing to grant their validity. If I say I am, then we have reached agreement, agreement on everlasting principles, and I am no relativist. If I choose to be a consistent relativist, of course, then I have to renounce those and all other permanent moral principles. But then, I have no right to object to your attempts, or the Moral Majority's, or Hitler's, to impose values on me. If imposing values is one of the things you like to do, just because it really feels good and right to you to impose values on others, then, according to subjective relativism, it's obviously right, for you, to impose values on me, and I have no grounds for protest. So this relativism, morality relativized to the individual, fails on either count. If I try to defend it on account of the values it defends, I cease to be a relativist, and if I try to be a consistent relativist, I lose all purchase on the field of ethics, including the right to resist the tyrant's imposition of values, which was the purpose for which I first advanced subjective relativism. To defend the individualism that the position sets out to exemplify, we must recover the commitments to reason, and to impartial consideration, with which we started.

Chapter 2
The Principles of Ethics

The occasion for the formulation of the generally accepted principles of ethics was a series of politically sensitive scandals, all in the early 1970s. The medical profession was stunned by a 1966 article in the prestigious *New England Journal of Medicine* by anesthesiologist Henry K. Beecher, "Ethics and Clinical Research," in which the author documented repeated abuse and deception of patients in the name of the scientific search for knowledge—experimentation with human beings. Then there was the exposure of the Tuskegee Study (of untreated syphilis in African American men), which emerged in the Associated Press in 1972, a study also conducted to find out more about the course of the disease, quite without the consent of the patients. (Nine years later the report came out in book form, in James Jones' *Bad Blood.*) Then came the famous (or infamous) Supreme Court Decision, Roe v. Wade, in 1973, and almost immediately reports began to circulate about gruesome experiments performed on fetal remains. When Caroline Kennedy, daughter of President John Kennedy, joined the demonstrators picketing the White House demanding an end to the fetal experiments, Congress knew that the time had come to act. It announced that all these abuses would immediately be dealt with, and formed a committee, the National Commission for the Protection of Human Subjects of Biomedical and Behavioral Research, to draw up regulations to govern all conduct of clinical research. The Commission was composed of many of the best scholars of religion, ethics and medicine in the country, and was given a free hand. Congress stipulated that the members must be drawn from different backgrounds and persuasions, to ensure that all voices in the national moral chorus were heard; somewhat to the surprise of the academics observing the process, the members did their work thoroughly and well.

How had they avoided the conflict invited by their ideological diversity, and managed to work together so well? The Commission realized early in its deliberations that they had no common history of ethical conviction on which to draw, so they homed in (according to one of their chroniclers, Stephen Toulmin) on the material that had inspired their creation: cases of clinical research that potentially or actually posed ethical problems. "The Case Method," we call it in the

L. Newton, *Ethical Decision Making: Introduction to Cases and Concepts in Ethics,* SpringerBriefs in Ethics, DOI: 10.1007/978-3-319-00167-8_2, © The Author(s) 2013

classroom, and it works by analogy. When we find a case on whose merits we can all agree—it was right, or it was wrong—we plant it in the middle of the ethical field, and as each succeeding case comes along we look for parallels and dissonances. By this method, according to the accounts, they concluded a series of reports on the conditions of permissibility of research with children, fetuses, those institutionalized as mentally infirm, and several other categories. At the end of it all, they gathered—in California, or possibly in Massachusetts, reports differ— to ask themselves what justifications they had used in fact, to reach their conclusions—to what principles had they in fact appealed in deciding ethical questions. The principles they came up with were individual autonomy (the consent of the subject of the research was essential, and the subject could not be deceived), nonmaleficence (The subject must not be harmed by the research), beneficence (the research had to be directed to a worthwhile purpose), and justice (the benefits of the research had to be widely applicable, and the subjects must not be taken only from disadvantaged populations—the Tuskegee experiments were clearly at the top of their minds).

These principles have wider justifications than the fact that very good ethicists came up with them in the late 1970s in Massachusetts or California. Consider: Ethics is about human beings. The values that we have appealed to quite uncritically in the preceding stories—values of rescue for the distressed, of fair treatment, of neighborhood peace and respect for rights—are not arbitrary or merely conventional. We can discover their foundations in the life of the human being, and derive them from fundamental aspects of human nature. The human being, and human nature, are endlessly complex, of course; yet the human being is universally recognizable to others of the species, and their preferences are very generally predictable. So if we avoid the complexities of the outer limits of human potentiality, it should be possible to say enough about the fundamentals of human morality just from the easily discoverable truths about the human being. The discussion links in a fairly straightforward way with the major ethical orientations which philosophers have, through our history, adopted, as reflective of these most basic moral principles (The discussion that follows recapitulates the discussion in the Introduction).

Then what are human beings about? Given the normative premise, that moral principle must be appropriate to human life if they are to govern human life, three basic, simple, readily observable facts about human beings determine the structure of our moral obligations:

2.1 Beneficence: People are Embodied

People are animals. They have bodies. They are matter; they exist in time and space and are subject to physical laws. These bodies are organic processes, requiring regular sustenance internally, and suffering all manner of slings and arrows of violent change externally. They experience pain, deprivation, and danger. They are prone to periodic failure unpredictably and to ultimate failure inevitably; they are mortal.

Then people have needs that must be satisfied if they are to survive. They need at least food, water, and protection from the elements and natural enemies. That means that they must control the physical environment to make from it the means to those ends. Failure to do so will lead quickly to pain and suffering. These are inevitable in any case; in this way we are reminded of our mortality.

The first and immediate implication for ethics is that, if we have any reason to care about human beings, then the relief of that suffering and the satisfaction of those needs should be our first concern. In philosophical terms, human need and vulnerability to harm give rise to duties of compassion (for suffering), non-maleficence (avoiding harm), and more generally, beneficence: working to satisfy human need, maximize human happiness, optimize human interests in all respects.

In general, the moral reasoning that takes help and harm to human beings as the primary determinant of the rightness of action is called "utilitarianism," following John Stuart Mill's description of that reasoning. (Mill 1859)

2.2 Justice: People are Social

Social animals regularly live in large groups of their own kind (i.e., in groups containing several to many active adult males); individuals raised apart from such groups exhibit behavior that is, and they are themselves, abnormal for the species. Whatever problems, therefore that people have with their physical environment they will have to solve in groups. They will soon discover that this necessity produces a new set of problems; they must cope with a social environment as well as the physical one. That social environment produces two further needs: for a social structure to coordinate social efforts, and for a means of communication adequate to the complex task of such coordination. The need for communication is fulfilled by the evolution of language.

The implication for ethics is that, given that there are so many of us, we must take account of each other in all our actions. We come saddled by nature with obligations, to the group in general and to other members of the group in particular, that we cannot escape or evade. Normal people (not psychopaths) seem to know this without being told. By nature human beings try, most of the time, to do good and avoid evil, in advance of knowing just what counts as good or evil. The attempt to do good, to others as to oneself, involves the adoption of "the moral point of view," or a stance of impartiality with regard to the distribution of benefits and burdens. Fairness, or justice, demands that we subject our actions to rule, and that the rule be the same for all who are similarly situated. What will make an act "right," ultimately, is not just that it serves individual happiness but that it serves the whole community; people are equal, and since equality is itself a value (derived from "equal dignity") the society must deal with them equally unless good reason is given for differential treatment.

Two philosophers who took Justice as central to their understanding of ethics were R. Edward Freeman of the University of Virginia, author of Stakeholder Theory, and the late John Rawls of Harvard University, whose landmark book on the subject he summarized in two simple principles, which he argued would provide the foundation of a just society:

Liberty: each person shall enjoy the greatest liberty compatible with a like liberty for all;
Difference: Equality of positions shall be maintained, unless it can be shown that

1. the creation of the inequality is advantageous for everyone (not just the ruling elite, not just the majority) especially the least advantaged;
2. the positions so created are open to all on the basis of equal opportunity. (John Rawls 1970)

2.3 Respect for Personal Autonomy: People are Rational

Normal adult human beings are able to consider abstract concepts, use language, and think in terms of categories, classes and rules. Since Immanuel Kant, we have recognized three categories of thought that characterize the way human beings deal with the objects and events of the world. These are time (when did something happen? in the past, the present, the future; and how long did it take? duration); space (where is some object? or how far away is it? location, bulk, distance); and causation (how did something happen? what brought it about? antecedents, agencies, powers, consequences). "Rationality," of course, in our ordinary discourse, means a good deal more than the basic ability to think in terms of when, where and how. Ordinarily we use the word to distinguish calm and dispassionate decision making from "emotional" or disorganized decision making; we use it to distinguish people capable of making good decisions from people who are not. But for our purposes here, we need go no further with the word. The creature that is "rational" will think, on occasion, in general terms, about classes and laws, extending over time, space, and possibility, while the creature that is "not rational" will think, if at all, only about particular (individual) objects or events.

Since people are rational, they can make rational choices. When people think about action they think in terms of classes of acts as well as individual acts. For instance, if my neighbor has a particularly attractive knife, and I desire to take it from him, and am currently making plans to do so, I shall make my plans based on what I already know about all cases of people taking things from other people. And I can contemplate not only those past acts of taking, and the present plan to take that knife, but all cases that will ever be of taking, especially of knives—future acts as well as past and present acts. But in that case I am thinking of action not yet taken, of action therefore undetermined, for which real alternatives exist. Since people can conceive of alternatives, they can choose among them—having thought over the circumstances, and deliberated on the outcomes, they can decide what to do. Put another way: I do not have to take that knife, if I have not yet done it. People are free, as we say, or autonomous moral agents. But then they can also realize that they could have done differently—I did not have to take the knife, and given my neighbor's understandable grief and anger at its loss, maybe I should not have. That is, I can feel guilt and remorse and assume responsibility for having chosen as I did.

As far as we know, we are alone among the animals in possession of this ability. Since people can conceive of classes of acts for which alternatives exist, they can make laws to govern acts in the future, specifying that the citizens (or whoever may be bound by the law) ought to act one way rather than another. No one, for instance, ought to take things that do not belong to them, and such takings, henceforth to be called "theft," shall be collectively punished. General obligations can be formulated and articulated for a whole society. Collectively (acting in their groups), people make collective choices, especially choices of rules, rather than relying on instinct; and they are then collectively responsible for those choices and individually responsible for abiding by them.

Rationality's implication for ethics is that, as freedom of choice is the characteristic that sets humans apart from the other animals, if we have any duty to respect human beings at all, it is this choice that we must respect. Persons are categorically different from the things of the physical world. They have dignity, inherent worth, rather than mere price or dollar value; they are bearers of rights and subjects of duties rather than mere means to our ends or obstacles to our purposes. Our duty of respect for persons, or respect for persons as autonomous beings, requires that we allow others to be free, to make their own choices and live their own lives; especially, we are required not to do anything to them without their consent.

Just as utilitarianism makes human happiness central to ethics, and the Rawlsian account of fairness makes justice central, a complete theoretical account of ethics can follow from the value of human autonomy. The philosopher most identified with the centrality of autonomy and moral agency to ethical theory is Immanuel Kant (Kant 1785).

2.4 The Human Condition

In summary: By 3, above, humans have minds, or as the philosophers call it, a rational nature; and by 1, above, humans have an apparently limitless capacity for physical and psychological suffering. Rationality and suffering are not found together anywhere else; possibly the angels have the first, and surely all beasts possess the second, but only human beings appear to be able to reflect upon their own suffering and contemplate the suffering of others of their kind, and that sets them apart from all creation. By virtue of rationality, human persons possess dignity and command respect. Ultimately, that respect entails the willingness to let other people make their own choices, develop their own moral nature, and live their lives in freedom. By virtue of that abysmal capacity for suffering, the human condition cries out for compassion and compels attention to human well-being and the relief of pain. And by 2, above, this condition is shared; we are enjoined not only to serve human need and respect human rights, but to establish justice by constructing a political and legal structure which will distribute fairly the burdens and benefits of life on this earth in the society of humans. These most general concepts: human welfare, human justice, and human dignity—are the source and criteria for evaluation of every moral system authored by human beings.

The same concepts are the source of every moral dilemma. Attention to human welfare requires us to use the maximization of human happiness (for the greatest number of individuals) as our criterion of right action. Attention to the needs of groups, and of social living, requires us to set fairness for all above benefit for some as our criterion. Yet duty can require that we set aside both the feelings of the groups and the happiness of the individual in the name of respect for human dignity. To protect the welfare of many it is often necessary to limit the liberty of the individual (the liberty to operate dangerous or noisy vehicles without a license, for instance). On the small scale as well as the large, to respect the liberty of persons is not always to further their best interests, when they choose against those interests (for instance, by taking addictive drugs or by spending themselves into debt). To maintain a rough equality among persons, it is often necessary to put unequal demands on the interests of some of them (by progressive taxation, for example). To preserve the community, it is sometimes necessary to sacrifice the interests of the few—but that course seems to discount the worth of the few, and so to violate justice.

2.5 The Basic Imperatives

Such conflict is fundamental to ethics, and is the major reason why ethics is famous as the discipline that has no clear answers. The human being is a complex creature, and when we extract human values from that complexity, we find them logically independent at the least, and often in opposition. There are, by tradition, two ways to formulate the opposition:

1. As a conflict of *values*: A value is a desired state, which we try, in our dealings, to advance or enhance or promote. The concepts so far discussed can be treated as values that are difficult to pursue simultaneously—the happiest society, the fairest or most equal society, the most free society or the lifestyle incorporating the most freedom.
2. As a conflict of *imperatives*: An imperative prescribes a duty to do or to forbear. It is occasionally more useful to see ethical conflict as a conflict of injunctions or prescriptions telling us what to do in any given situation. We are told—by the Law and the Prophets, by our religion, by our parents, by our employers, by

the civil law—that we must respect the rights of others, be fair to everyone, and serve each other's needs. Sometimes it is not possible to do everything at once.

Over against every clear value, there is another value, which sometimes conflicts. Over against every clear imperative, there is a contrary imperative, equally clear, which sometimes applies. Ethics is the discipline that derives these values and imperatives, works out the consequences of our efforts to protect them, and musters what light it can to show us the possible reconciliations and the necessary compromises that attend their application in practice.

The terms "principle," "imperative," and "value" are sometimes used interchangeably. We will attempt to use "concept" to mean the principle in the form of a definition, as above; "value" as a desired end-state, to be achieved or enhanced; "imperative" as a prescription of duty. Morality is sometimes best understood as a system of imperatives, and generally imperatives are cited as the basis for the conclusions of applied ethics. Thus the three concepts (welfare, justice and dignity) correspond to the three fundamental imperatives—beneficence, justice and respect for persons.

1.   Centering on welfare: Do No Harm, and Where Possible Do Good: Because we must live, and because we can suffer, we must value life and happiness: safety, protection from harm, absence of pain, hunger or suffering of any kind; enjoyment, pleasure. That is, we have an obligation to help and protect each other, to relieve suffering, to choose each action, or rule of action, according to the amount of pain it will relieve or happiness it will provide. This general duty we call **beneficence,** or concern for welfare.

This imperative is often broken down into four logically related but different prescriptions:

   a.   Do no harm (the duty of **non-maleficence**): In the pattern of duties to do good and to avoid harm, this duty is the negative, individual, and immediate part. (For instance: no matter how much fun it would be, do not blow up the bridge).
   b.   Prevent harm wherever possible (the duty of prudence, or stewardship): this duty generalizes the one before, enjoining us to attempt to keep agencies besides ourselves from doing harm (If the bridge is near collapse, act to shore it up and keep people off it until it is fixed.)
   c.   Remedy harm wherever possible (the duty of compassion or charity): this duty is the proactive equivalent of the two before, enjoining concern for suffering and positive efforts to relieve it (If the bridge has collapsed, pull the people out of the water, even if you don't know them and have no other obligations to them).
   d.   Do good, provide benefit, wherever possible (Build better bridges).

Note that in this pattern of duties, the duty of non-maleficence takes moral priority (i.e., if you can provide benefit to many people, only at the cost of doing harm to a few, there is a presumption against doing whatever would result in the benefit and harm). The second two follow from the same presumption, and the last

comes into play only when the others are taken care of. The priority of non-maleficence can, of course, be overridden, as when the state takes my property to build
a road, doing harm to me in order to do good for many; but it can only do so on
proper authority, with at least an attempt to provide compensation, and on presen-
tation of compelling reasons.

2. Centering on Justice: Observe the Requirements of Fair Dealing: Because we
    must live together, we must adhere to rules of equal treatment, justice, fair-
    ness, and rule of law (equality before the law); trust and trustworthiness,
    honesty in word and deed. Then we have an obligation to acknowledge our
    membership in, and dependence on, the human community and the commu-
    nity in which we live—to contribute to its life, obey its laws, customs and
    policies, to be honest in all our dealings with our fellows and above all to hold
    ourselves accountable to them for our actions, especially as they affect others.
    This duty we call **justice.**
    This duty also has recognizable sub-imperatives:

    a. Obey the law and the codes of your profession. All are equally bound
        by these general prescriptions, and it is not fair to make an exception of
        yourself. Also, as possible: take responsibility for enforcement.
    b. Treat all groups alike: do not condition treatment of persons on their
        membership in a favored group. This is the duty of non-discrimination, or
        provision of equal opportunity.
    c. Act affirmatively to remedy the results of past injustices; wherever pos-
        sible, seek out the least advantaged and the previously excluded for occu-
        pation of preferred posts.
    d. Recognize merit; treat people as they deserve to be treated based on what
        they have done or merited. Included in this general duty is the more per-
        sonal duty of gratitude.

3. Centering on dignity: Respect Persons (as autonomous beings): Because we
    aspire to the full potential of humanity, we must value freedom. We take lib-
    erty, autonomy, rationality to be ideals, and value them in others as much as
    we prize our own. The human enterprise is an endless quest to become better,
    wiser, more loving people, and we must cultivate people and institutions that
    will protect that quest. We have an obligation to respect the choices of oth-
    ers, to allow them the space to live their lives, to the end, the way they see fit.
    For ourselves, we have the obligation to realize our own potential, not only to
    discern for ourselves the moral course of action, and to take responsibility for
    the moral choices we make, but to extend our knowledge and the scope of our
    reason to become as fully as possible the autonomous persons we are capable
    of being. This duty we call **respect for persons.**
    Again, more specific duties can be derived from Respect:

    a. Tell the truth: the duty of veracity or truth telling is primarily derived
        from the duty to enhance autonomy by making rational decision possible.

No person can act rationally if denied the truth. From this duty we derive the requirement of informed consent in the health care professions, and the duty of full disclosure in law and business.

b. Celebrate differences, whether individual or cultural. Create a positive atmosphere for the developing of idiosyncratic lifestyles that fulfill individual needs and preferences—as long as they violate no one else's rights.

Clearly none of these imperatives is optional. We cannot choose not to have bodies. We cannot choose not to need each other, and although we may sometimes wish we could, we cannot choose not to choose, not to be free. And these imperatives are logically independent one from another. They can conflict. All ethical dilemmas follow from that fact.

2.6 Some Cases to Illustrate the Dilemmas

Let's consider some of the problematic instances. How do we balance beneficence, the greatest happiness for the greatest number, for instance, with the requirement of honesty, which is a moral imperative based on individual integrity? Central moral values, like the requirements above, of integrity, reason and impartiality, precede ethics. One of my colleagues suggested the following case, based on a real event:

2.6.1 End of Year Bonus

The last day of school before Christmas break was also Mary Kantarian's last shot at making sure she qualified for her top bonus level award. She was having a great year as the Northeast regional manager for the educational division of Delphi Technology. Delphi's new multimedia programs were immensely popular with secondary school educators across the country. As the year was closing down, Mary had converted all of her current sales leads to meet her year-end sales goal of $1,000,000. At least that's what she thought as she contacted her sales manager, Dave Jennings, on her cell phone.

"You are still $1,000 short of the bonus level," Dave reported. "I just received your latest net sales printout and that's where you stand. Unless we receive a minimum order from your territory before the end of the year, it looks like you'll miss out on your $10,000 bonus award for reaching the million dollar mark."

Just $1,000 short! What a bad break! Sure, her regular commissions on her sales added up to a respectable annual salary, but the $10,000 bonus award was what she was counting on to help meet the down payment on the new home she and her husband had been trying to finance for several years.

With just a few hours left before the close of the school day—and the end of her sales quota period—Mary had what appeared to be a solution just a few blocks away. The head of the social studies department at Lincoln High School loved Delphi's programs, but beleaguered Lincoln High had no funds available. Many students attending this inner-city school had to share textbooks! A call to the school earlier in the day revealed that the money situation hadn't changed.

But—why not just pay for the program herself? Mary could provide the money for a minimum $1,000 order right now to the school so the department head could issue a purchase requisition today! The school would gain an immensely valuable educational program and she would meet her coveted million dollar sales quota. (And earn $10,000 on a worthy investment of $1,000.) Surely—this is a win–win situation. Or is it?

It does not appear that the company intended to reward this type of behavior when they set the incentives for their salespeople! But it is Mary's own money. Does the dishonesty involved in sending in these new sales figures outweigh the rewards for the company, the school—and Mary? It sounds like a good deal: everyone wins, no one is hurt, and as for the source of that money, no one's the wiser. It might be noted that that is precisely the sort of thinking that led to many of the worst business scandals of the last decades.

Let's take another conflict, this time between another permanent value, the value of human life, and the imperative of beneficence.

2.6.2   Baby Samantha

Baby Samantha was born with staggering injuries to her nervous system. The skull lay open, at birth, to the air; the brain was largely outside the skull. There was no obvious way to get it back in, had any been motivated to try, which no one was. So situated, the brain was not connected with any sensory organs, or indeed with most of the rest of the body. The brain stem was intact, so the child was breathing, but there was no other role for that detached organ.

The physicians met with Carol, Samantha's mother. They explained the devastating nature of the baby's injuries, and told her that she was free to choose that no further medical intervention would be employed. The baby would be kept comfortable until she died. Carol insisted that her religion forbade her to "choose death," and that the baby should be given "every chance" at life. Surgeons reluctantly amputated the portion of the brain irrevocably outside the skull, and placed the baby on life support (feeding tubes, antibiotics, and anti-seizure drugs.) When it became clear that no further medical treatment would help her, she was moved to the Sycamores Home for the Elderly and Long-Term Care Facility, run by the Town of Belleville and currently administered by Director Geoffrey Baumgartner. She was to be left there until she died.

Four years later, the child is still alive. Her management has become a nightmare to the staff and especially to Geoff Baumgartner. What's left of her brain has constant seizures. The sites of the connections to her body of the tubes that bring food into her stomach and carry away her wastes are continually infected. She's received so many antibiotics that they have little effect anymore, so the Home has to use more and more expensive ones. Her mother, who still visits now and again, and insists, contrary to fact, that she sees responses from her daughter, is penniless, so the only support is from Medicaid. Medicaid doesn't begin to reimburse the expensive medication, let alone the endless labor of caring for the child. Samantha is the cause and center of two ongoing crises: the crisis in staff morale resulting from the apparently fruitless task of "tending this vegetable," and the financial crisis of the Home, bad enough in any case, that Samantha makes dramatically worse. It's Geoff's job to manage both crises, and he doesn't think he's doing a very good job.

"Can't we just stop pumping antibiotics into her and let her die?" one of the nurses asks him. Geoff had already asked the Home's lawyer about that, and been told that there are no direct precedents, but probably not. The mother has threatened that she will sue the facility for neglect should the child die, on grounds that Samantha is a Disabled Person under the Aid for Disabilities Act, and therefore deserves every effort to preserve her life—or, "life," you might want to say. On the other hand, what judge would impute malice if Samantha simply died of a runaway infection?

What should Geoff do?

This case is not unusual for any hospital or long-term care Home that shelters impaired infants. Agonizing decisions are made every day, attempting to balance the interest in preserving the infant's life (which is what they were set up to do) with the equally strong imperative not to allow unnecessary suffering. Prolonging life with no sentience, or quality of life for the infant, and with a grim prognosis for any future, is not generally held to be morally obligatory, and the parent's interest in keeping the child alive is not supposed to weigh in the balance at all. But in this area, the law—rather, the possible outcome of any lawsuit—is uncertain, the mother's love is clearly genuine, the financial problems of the Home (which are also not supposed to weigh in the decision at all) are serious, and the dilemma facing the administrator of the Home is real. No simple appeal to clear and accepted values will solve his problem here.

In both cases above, the universal ethical imperative of beneficence is set against a primary moral commitment, one that costs us dearly to ignore. When the issues become more complex, we can see the three basic imperatives set against each other. Consider the following case, hypothetical in this version but based on numerous real ones.

2.6.3   The Alcoholic in the Workplace

(Note: this case demonstrates the peculiar intractability of this type of ethical dilemma. In the "A" portion of the case, the three major principles suggested by your text are in direct opposition. In the "B" portion, the arguments for **both** sides are drawn from the **same** principles, not because the principles mean nothing or the participants are arguing incorrectly, but simply because our calculations of benefit are necessarily speculative, our assessments of justice depend on the framework adopted, and our respect for human dignity can be expressed in one of several ways.)

A. An Employee with a Problem

A tense meeting in the office of Mr. R. Howard Williams, Vice President for Personnel (Howie, in what follows), on the case of Mr. Francis J. O'Brien, Director of Special Accounts, Finance Department (Frank), on the request of Mr. Joseph Machowski, Vice President for Finance (Joe), of the Allbest Engineering Division. All three parties are present.

Howie: (after good mornings, offerings of coffee etc.) Joe, you're the "complainant," as it were, why don't you present the complaint.

Joe: Sure. Frank and I have been working together, more or less, for over seven years now, and I have a great deal of respect for him as a person, Frank, I want to say that right now. But in the last seven or eight months there's been nothing but trouble, and if it were up to me we'd have let you go by now, I guess you know that. There was the time in April when we needed the data on the Stoddard account for the planning meeting, and it was your responsibility to get it there, and you were nowhere to be found, and neither was the data. Then there were the long lunch hours that we only found out about when your secretary was sick and the substitute found out that she was supposed to cover for you from one to two-thirty in the afternoon! Whatever else you can do with secretaries in these liberated days, you can't ask them to lie for you—it's just not fair. Then you were due for the

And speaking of "sick," you've missed six Mondays, out "sick", out of the last four-teen. Someone has to do your work when you're out, you know. You are just not carrying your share of the load. You missed the July 1 Department Report deadline, Howie, I've got all this in black and white. I spoke to you about the Stoddard account, and when I found out about the lunch hours I put a disciplinary note in your file. Another went in after you missed the May meeting, and a final warning after July 1. After I noticed the Monday pattern I started to process the papers for termination, and found out I had to go through this office, not my choice. That's why we're here.

Howie: That's **one** of the reasons why we're here. Joe, as a good supervisor, you have documented performance and stopped there. But I have to look into causes and cures. I know you've been happy with Frank's work in the past, and that you would be happy to keep him on if he could be restored to full performance. I also know that it would cost the company almost $100,000, all things considered, to separate Frank, hire a successor, and train him or her to do Frank's job. And I suspect that Frank would rather keep his job than be fired! So we serve everyone's interests if we get Frank working well again. And I think we can do that.

Frank, I know some things that Joe does not. Two of your co-workers have come to me, independently, worried about your drinking. Your neighbor Walter, who plays tennis with me, has mentioned his concern over the times you've arrived home clearly under the influence of alcohol, once driving over a corner of his lawn. His wife noticed alcohol on your breath at a neighborhood meeting two months ago. And our health center's part time medical staff member circulated a set of physical symptoms of alcohol abuse—including mottled face and hands—that describe you to a T. Now wait a minute, before you get mad, I know full well that none of this is "evidence" that would stand up in court. But court is not my concern. I want to help you and help the company at the same time. You probably know already that you're in a pattern of alcohol abuse that can land you out of a job, out of health, out of life. This is probably a part of other troubles, including the problems with your wife that you've told some of us about. No we are not spying! The only reason I listen to this "gossip" is so that, sometimes, I can help. We have rehabilitation programs for immediate help, family therapy to help both you and your wife get a better grip on your problems, and connections with Alcoholics Anonymous and Alanon for long term support. Listen to me, Frank. You, your family, and the company will all get through this in decent shape if you will let us help you.

Frank: Finally I get a word in edgewise? Thanks. I have very little to say. Joe, you and I have not gotten along, and it's not entirely your fault. I thought when I joined on here that the Finance division was a short assignment until a position opened up in Marketing, where I can use some creativity in my job. I've repeatedly put in for the switch but no one can quite find the way to get me over there. I'm sorry if my work doesn't seem to be a model of good attitude, but that's why. And when you look at all the stuff you've got in black and white, there really isn't much there. I did miss a dead-line or two, but every one of my counterparts in other Departments has, too. You guys call these meetings out of the blue, demand full reports from all of us, and then get all huffy when we can't supply them just like that. Sorry about that missed meeting; you have me dead to rights there. I just forgot about it. One meeting in nine years? And you were going to fire me? I think after nine years I deserve an occasional long lunch, and if you believe that secretarial scuttlebutt about "forcing me to lie for him," you're dumber than I think. As for the Mondays, I have a nasty case of gastroenteritis that has a way of flaring up after a weekend's eating and drinking; sorry about that too. Yes, drinking, Howie, and whatever you may have heard from the nosy neighbors, I'm not a drunk, and I have problems enough without well-intentioned busybodies trying to reform my life for me. I value my privacy, and my freedom to choose my own lifestyle, and I think, as an adult, I'm entitled to them. What I do on my own time is my own affair. I may change the medication for the gastroenteritis, or I may not. I will try not to be late or absent any more. But you don't have enough in that file to fire me, and you don't have any right to run my life for me, no matter what your opinions of me may be. I'd appreciate it if you'd leave me alone.

Who's right?

Incidentally, Frank did, eventually, opt for the rehabilitation route. That was not the end of the story. It continues in what follows.

B. A Case for the Corporate Ethics Committee of Allbest's Engineering Division (AED)

Mr. R. Howard Williams, Vice President of Personnel (Howie in what follows), presenting the case to the committee: Gentlemen, thank you for agreeing to help us decide this case. It concerns the Director of Special Accounts in the Finance Department, Francis J. O'Brien, who has been with the company for a little over nine years. Frank was diagnosed alcoholic about a year ago, went through a course of rehabilitation at our expense, seemed all right and returned to work; now he's drinking again. He's been suspended without pay for one week, by which time we have to decide whether to put him through rehabilitation again or terminate his employment here for good. As you may know, this case has been placed before your committee at the request of Robbins Brown, President of this Division, and…

Mr. Joseph Machowski, Vice President of Finance (Joe in what follows), interrupting: Howie, can we make this quick? I've got two more meetings this morning and a desk full of work.

Howie: OK, Joe, why don't you go first? You're Frank's direct superior, after all.

Joe: Thanks, I guess. I am not, for starters, familiar with this procedure. We have here a case of a bad actor, we've done everything we can for him, and why Rob Brown wants you to get involved in the case is beyond me. Anyway, Frank was hired nine years ago to fill a low-level vacancy in the finance department. He's pretty good with numbers and in a few years was promoted to credit manager. He was perfectly competent to manage the accounts, but couldn't get along with his supervisor, so we moved him into an auditing position. He claimed that with his winning personality he should be in marketing, but Sandy Levine, then VP of Finance, argued that his talents seemed better suited to finance, so he stayed in our division. When we promoted him to Director of Special Accounts, he still said he wanted to be in marketing, but there wasn't a position open. In his present job he has a lot of freedom of action, so I'm not on top of how his performance went from day one, but about a year and a half ago it started to go directly down hill—missed deadlines, missed meetings, absenteeism, just very poor. Disciplinary notices didn't do too much good. Eventually Howie got hold of the case, got the Employee Assistance counselors involved, and they made some progress: he admitted he'd been drinking a lot and agreed to go into a detox and rehab program, followed up with AA meetings, get the family in on it, all that stuff. Well, it worked for awhile, then he started fighting with his wife again, missed a couple of reports, refused to admit there was anything wrong when I called him on them, then showed up in the office drunk after lunch on Tuesday. That was the last straw. We sent him home then and there and notified him of the suspension the next day. Now what do we do with him? I say fire him:

1. He's not doing his work so everybody else has to do it. It's not fair to the others, who are pulling their share of the load, to ask them to pull his too. Furthermore, we've given him one good chance to pull himself out of it, more than we've given others. He doesn't deserve any more indulgence.
2. Keeping him would be bad for the company. The work we expect him to do is not being done well, he's demoralizing the other employees, and it's too expensive to try to drag him out of the gutter again. We do have the welfare of the company to think of, you know.
3. It isn't even good for him to keep him—it's pretending he's not a responsible adult. We told him we'd fire him if he started drinking again, he started, now we ought, just on principle, to do what we said we'd do. He's a grownup now, he's responsible for his behavior, and we shouldn't treat him like a child or an imbecile.

So I say he goes, period. Now, if you'll excuse me, I'm off to the next meeting.

Howie: Thanks, Joe. Donna, why don't you take the story from here? Donna Reed is our substance abuse counselor.

Donna: You have to try to understand the situation from Frank's point of view. He's been here for nine years, he's undoubtedly done a good job—his file is full of commendations, up until the last few years—but he hasn't gotten into the department he wants, and he thinks his talents are not being fully used. He was saddled with an incompetent supervisor for awhile, and still resents that. Maybe he could have been more philosophical about his treatment by the company—but then his wife started bugging him about how he should get promoted faster, and should make more money, and he found himself torn between his loyalty to the company and his loyalty to his family. Then his teenagers had problems and that was worrying him too. The drinking didn't seem so serious to him—just a temporary reaction to stress—but he was willing to try rehabilitation, and did, and it seemed to work. If his wife hadn't started in on him again, he might have stayed sober indefinitely. But she's been working with Alanon counselors recently, and she and Frank both think that a short stay in that rehab center will get him back on his feet for good this time. I think it's very hopeful, and I think the committee ought to advise sending him back to the center. What do you think, Mr. Williams?

Howie: I think I'm with you, Donna. The way I see it, we're responsible for the man. Nine years isn't a whole life, but it's a sizable chunk out of a manager's career. We had to have known how much it frustrated him to be kept where we could use him, in the finance department, not in marketing where he wanted to be. We let this behavior start, and let it go because we were too busy to catch it, and now I think we owe him that second chance:

1. It's only fair: we profited from his work when he did well, now we owe at least that second mile. Just because he's in trouble, and his family is going through a troublesome phase, doesn't mean we can toss him overboard; surely he deserves better of us.
2. It's the best course for the bottom line. Sure, while he's drinking he's costing us money. But do you know what it would cost to train a successor? It's been shown that rehabilitating an alcoholic, at least at the management level, costs only 1/17 as much as totally replacing him. With that kind of return, it's worth risking the investment of one more course of treatment.
3. He's a human being. If he loses his job, for drinking, he'll lose the last shred of self-respect he has. He'll never get another job at the level he deserves, or stop drinking, and I don't know what will happen to his family. You just can't treat a human life that way.

All right, gentlemen, there is the issue as we see it. Donna and I will return to our offices and leave you to your deliberations. Let us know what you decide.

No one principle, no one form of ethical reasoning is inherently superior to the others. We may use them all, and usually, in the course of a discussion involving ethics, we do. But it is important to note the differences among them, for if we do not, we condemn ourselves to talk past each other and frustrate our dialogue. We saw one example of this frustration in the debate between the operators of the abortion clinic and the angry neighbors, in the third case above: the physicians were arguing consequentially, in terms of the objectives achieved, and the neighbors were arguing non-consequentially, in terms of the nature of the actions themselves. As a result, each regarded the others' arguments as simply irrelevant to the main problem. For another example, at a dinner party some years ago, I came across a heated debate on the problem of educating inner-city African American teenagers. One side of the debate was arguing that African Americans had been treated so badly in the past, and had been denied such basic amenities and encouragement, that it was unjust to expect them to measure up to middle-class educational expectations. The other side, made up of schoolteachers, was arguing that education provided the only decent prospects for the future, and indeed, the only way out of the ghetto, for these youngsters, and unless they got their act together and got motivated somehow to finish school, the next generation would be just as disadvantaged and ill-treated as the present one.

Were these two groups really arguing against each other? No. Each could easily have conceded the other's point (and sometimes did) while maintaining its own. Rather, they were arguing *past* each other, one arguing consequentially (toward the future, bleak or somewhat brighter, depending on the means, especially educational means, adopted now), and the other deontologically (from justice). Both, by the way, were making excellent points. You might want to warm up your minds at this point by joining that debate; but please, do a better job than they did at keeping straight what kind of argument you are using.

Chapter 3
Professional Ethics

3.1 What Constitutes a "Profession"?

A **profession** is, briefly, an occupational group distinguished from others by possession of a constellation of properties, more or less central to its operations.
  Professionals claim:

(a) The possession of **knowledge of an art**, or esoteric body of knowledge, scientific or otherwise, not easily acquired, imparted by a lengthy course of professional education, governed and evaluated by the professionals, through which the professionals exercise control over entry into the profession. The duty to advance the state of the art through research is part of a duty of gratitude, in appreciation of that education.

(b) A certain **dedication to service to clients**, persons who benefit directly from professional work, with whom the professional has a quasi-fiduciary relationship, which is protected by some form of professional-client privilege that ensures the maintenance of confidentiality of all dealings between professional and client.

(c) A certain **dedication to service to the public**, or the common good, from whose politics the professional is protected by professional autonomy, which entails that only peer review (review by other professionals) shall be used to evaluate professional conduct.

(d) A **professional creed or code of ethics** that binds the professionals to a certain standard of behavior.

(e) The **intention to make a living at what they do** (as distinct from amateurs in the field).

Every profession claims all of those to some degree, although each profession would put them in a different order of priority. Medicine, our paradigm profession, which has evolved as a consulting profession since the days of Hippocrates of Cos (500 BC) would put duty to the client, or patient, first, and others beneath it; but physicians also acknowledge the duty to do research and advance medical knowledge, to help run the medical schools, to contribute to public health, and to maintain the peer review system that protects professional autonomy.

By way of contrast, while the structure of the legal profession is much the same, their Code of Professional Conduct is not nine sentences long, but a whole volume—and it has the force of law. It is very clear in legal ethics, that the first duty is to the client—but the lawyer is also an officer of the court, leaving him in a dilemma if the client wants to tell lies on the witness stand.

Scholars, university professors, may put service to the body of knowledge in their field first among their obligations; yet they will protect and serve their students as clients, acknowledge an unwritten code of professional ethics, help to educate their graduate students, and protect their academic freedom, which guarantees professional autonomy.

Journalists may see the public at large as their primary client; policy analysts may serve government as its client, with the public (as distinct from the government) a distant second in its thoughts. In all professions, an ideal of service with integrity informs the professional practice of most of the practitioners. It is helpful to remember that the notion of "profession," like "vocation," came originally from those who chose to dedicate their lives to service in a religious order. Some professions took their initial guidance from religious orders (the Hippocratic Oath was the particular code of a religious order of physicians) or, like the priesthood, retain the relationship to this day. Professionals regard themselves, and are generally regarded, as a privileged group of initiates into private wisdom, bound to special laws and obligations that the lay public cannot understand, let alone enforce.

Whatever element each profession may place first in the constellation, the elements of a profession are tied together in a logically coherent pattern which is the same for all. Because the expertise of the professional field is esoteric, difficult and time-consuming to obtain, there is no point in putting laymen (non-professionals) in charge of evaluating professional practice; they simply won't understand it, and will not be able to tell whether or not it is being done well. Hence professional autonomy is a natural necessity, not some kind of dispensable privilege. Since professionals must operate autonomously, they are bound to a system of peer review according to a code of ethics, since otherwise there would be no standard at all by which their performance could be judged. And since only professionals can say what a professional ought to know, only professionals can run the professional educational system and determine which of its graduates are fit to practice the profession. A profession serves the common good, by participating in town committees and engaging in community education activities, but its primary service is through service to its clients, governed by a quasi-fiduciary obligation including the protection of confidentiality.

(By way of example: it is in the public interest that people who are sick should seek medical care, and that people who have violated the law should come forward and make restitution. But people who are frightened by the social implications of their disease or legal trouble may be unwilling to step forward unless they know that the information they give will not be shared with anyone, at least until they have agreed that it is in their interest to share it. Hence we protect confidentiality

between doctor and patient, lawyer and client, and by extension, priest and peni-
tent, teacher and student.)

Again, to protect the public interest, there are limits on the privilege of confidentiality: the client must be of age (limiting teachers in protecting information),
must not be currently engaged in fraud or other crime (which would activate a
"duty to warn" for the professional), and certain conditions may not be kept private no matter who the clients may be (venereal disease, gunshot wounds, and
child abuse, for instance).

The professional of any kind is committed to quality and integrity: he or she is
obliged to practice the art at its most advanced state, defend the honor of the profession (in part by helping to weed out the dishonorable members) and to advance
the state of the art through research, writing and teaching. All this takes time,
which is why a "professional" is one who works at the profession full time; no
profession worthy of the name can be done half-heartedly or half time.

3.2 Professional Ethics and Market Ethics

The professional ethic is anchored by the quasi-fiduciary obligation that the professional has toward his client—the obligation to make each decision for the client's interests and welfare, not the professional's own. Without this ethic, the very
notion of professional practice is impossible. By definition, the central characteristic of the profession is esoteric knowledge, beyond the ken of any layman. The
client comes to the professional because of needs that the client cannot satisfy on
his own because he, as a layman, lacks that knowledge: the patient comes to the
doctor because he does not know why he feels sick, the client comes to the lawyer
because he does not know enough of the law to know if he has a case against his
neighbor, or is in some kind of trouble with the law, or has the right to carry on
business as he plans.

He must trust the professional to use that esoteric knowledge to help him—at
least, to do no harm to him.

If the professional decides to use that knowledge, and that trust, to advance his
own interests at the expense of the client's (by telling a perfectly healthy woman
that she has a dangerous illness that will require expensive medicine made by the
physician, for instance; by telling the client that he's got a wonderful case against
his neighbor which the lawyer will be glad to pursue for a retainer of several thousand dollars, when no such case can be successful), every client would leave the
professional's office worse off than when he went in. By definition, the layman has
no way of evaluating the quality of the professional's advice; to know enough to
do that, he would have to be a professional himself. Were that the common experience, the custom of consulting professionals would rapidly pass out of existence.

The professional ethic, then, stands in distinct contradiction to the market ethic
for which Adam Smith argued. Adam Smith, the 18th century economist who
defined and defended the free market, believed that in the open market, if each

party looked after his own interests and his own interest only, the result would be the advancement of the common good. Therefore when dealing on the market, it is not only the right but the duty of merchant and customer alike to seek his own advantage, limited only by the requirements of honesty in representation of the goods, abstention from physical or psychological coercion, and fulfillment of contract.

The professional ethic is just the opposite: dealing with the client, the professional's first duty is to find out if the client needs professional services at all, and if not, to bid him farewell without taking a penny. His second duty is to arrange to serve a client who needs his service in such a way as to maximize the client's profit from the service while minimizing its cost. Again, the client will be unable to verify any of this, so if the professional decides to cheat the client, there is little likelihood of being found out—unless the cheating becomes habitual and the professional gets careless. To an astoundingly large extent, the viability of professional practice in the United States, for all professions, rests on the integrity of the individual practitioners, unmonitored by any but (informally) their peers.

The professional's third duty is to protect the client in the profit from that service by maintaining the strictest confidentiality concerning the identity of his clients and the nature of the services provided, despite temptations to serve his own advantage (financial or social) by revealing them.

3.3 Professionals in Business

Professions intersect with the larger business world in several ways. First, each professional is in business, in that as above, he expects to make a living practicing his profession. In the village economy of American history, the professional carried on a solo or partnership practice in towns and city neighborhoods, serving clients as they came in the door, billing them individually for services rendered. Medicine and law, the flagship professions, worked that way until very recently. In such cases, the determination of a fair fee was in part an individual matter, in part a community agreement that would probably, today, not pass anti-trust scrutiny. Professionals had always to resist the temptation to convince clients that more services were necessary than really were, and sometimes they succumbed to that temptation, especially when times were hard. But in the confines of town or neighborhood, it was difficult for professional greed to get out of hand; most of the restraints that worked on small businesses worked for the professionals.

But professionals also work within those businesses that require their expertise, as engineers within firms that produce highly technical products. Do the professionals' duties to adhere to the standards of their profession change at that point? Richard DeGeorge would argue that they do; that once the professional has tendered his advice to management, his duty is to support whatever decision management makes. Professionals do have the responsibility to make their views known to their employers, he insists, possibly (especially when public safety seems to be at risk) to argue that actions should be taken by management to further a goal held by the profession. But beyond that, "an engineering judgment, a legal judgment, and a medical judgment are only part of the relevant information that goes into a managerial judgment." [ ] (We recall the decision process that led to the launching of the ill-fated Challenger, where one of the corporate officers, who had started out as a practicing engineer, was told to "take off your engineering hat and put on your management hat"; he did, and cast the deciding vote in favor of launching.) DeGeorge's conclusion seems to contain significant risks, not only for engineers, but for all professions and the public at large.

Some professions, like nursing and engineering, were composed from their beginning primarily of practitioners employed in larger institutions, hospitals or corporations, who had to hammer out their claims to professional autonomy against the claims of their employers. As colleges and universities joined the scientific and commercial growth of post-War America, college professors joined the ranks of professionals worrying about autonomy while collecting significant paychecks. These "employed professionals" have had to negotiate the narrow channels of professional responsibility among the rocks of employer demands, and the negotiations are not always successful.

Consider, for instance: Should nurses join unions (organizations of employees formed to protect their material interests—wages, benefits, and job security— vis-à-vis the employers)? How does protection of nurse salaries fit with protection of the patient's interests? Could it ever be justifiable for nurses to go out on strike, leaving their patients untended? But if not, what power could the union have? The same question applies to the college professors.

On the other hand, should engineers leave the status of employee by joining management (corporate officers charged with protecting shareholder interests, in part by keeping employee demands to a minimum)? By doing that, do they not abandon the engineer's commitment to a quality product in favor of the management goal of cost-cutting?

More recently yet, even the flagship professions have found themselves caught up in corporate objectives. The "storefront law firms" have turned members of the legal profession into underpaid and overworked clerks with specialized knowledge, monitored by corporate managers for productivity and deprived of the autonomy to run each case as they see fit. In the Health Care area, the insurance companies that carry health care insurance now own many medical practices. This arrangement turns physicians into employees without protections: if a physician costs the practice too much in a given year, he or she can be separated from it and lose his or her entire practice. The conflict of interest built into this and similar arrangements is excruciating for physician and patient alike. To eliminate it, should we encourage physicians to join unions?

Chapter 4
Some Considerations from Moral Psychology

Among the initial distinctions that underlie the field of ethics is that between normative disciplines (the study of what should be done, of duties, rights, and obligations) and empirical disciplines (the study of what is in fact true about the world, as shown by observations on many levels). All the physical and social sciences are empirical disciplines. Can there be a "science" of morality? Apparently not; there are no facts **at all** which can tell us what should be done, without a normative premise. That is a logical truth; to deny it is to contradict oneself. But there can be sciences that surround and explain the manifestations of moral behavior (or lack of it) in the world, and some of these studies have been of interest to ethicists. It may be enlightening to tie together some reflections on the moral thought and behavior of human beings, if only to lay the groundwork for efforts to improve that moral thinking and acting in an increasingly disordered world.

4.1 Evolutionary Psychology: What Darwin Tells Us About How We Think

First of all, what do humans do **naturally**, prior to any teaching? Evolutionary biology is one of the few disciplines that can contribute to our understanding of the "natural" (unschooled) human. We know that in a world where a constant tendency to overpopulation (of all species) exists, some will survive and some will not, and those creatures whose genetic composition gives rise to traits that are best adapted to the environmental demands—say, longer necks on hoofed creatures like giraffes who live on the leaves of trees—will survive and pass those genes to the next generation. Shorter-necked giraffes may not. Over the generations, we will find giraffes with longer and longer necks (up to a point). But it is not enough to survive: the giraffe must also mate, produce offspring and raise those offspring to sexual maturity if the genes are to persevere for more than a generation. Giraffes disinclined to mate, or unable to raise offspring, will not supply genes to future generations. *On the hypothesis, or assumption,* that the survival of one's gene pool

L. Newton, *Ethical Decision Making: Introduction to Cases and Concepts in Ethics*, SpringerBriefs in Ethics, DOI: 10.1007/978-3-319-00167-8_4, © The Author(s) 2013

is a good thing, we are in a position to say that behavior that results in survival and successful propagation and rearing of offspring is **"right"** for any member of a species. As we sometimes put it, evolution **favors** behavior that is conducive to survival.; most behavior, and dispositions to behavior, have a genetic component, so survival-oriented behavior favors and preserves the genes of the group that engages in it. Just what is important to survival varies with the species and the circumstances.

Let's take a simple example.

Observation: When an adult healthy male lion comes upon a pride of lions not related to himself (a pride consists of a dominant male, several lionesses and their cubs), he tends to challenge the dominant male for possession of the pride. If he wins, he drives off the once-dominant male and proceeds to kill all the cubs. That brings all the lionesses into heat, so he mates them and thereafter protects them and their cubs from other male lions. Now, why does he do all that?

Simple explanation (say, for older children): The new lion wants to run the pride so that he can have cubs of his own, so he fights and beats the former lion, then kills the former lion's cubs and mates with the lionesses so they can bear his cubs. Simple, but of course it's a fairy tale; lions have no such plans, projects, or desires, let alone a concept of "cubs sired by another lion."

Better explanation: The male lion has a behavioral disposition, undoubtedly innate (how would he have *learned* it?), to do all those things; the objective result, no matter what he wants or intends, is that the cubs of that pride will have his genes rather than the former lion's. Since innate dispositions are encoded in the genes, there's a strong probability that his male cubs will have the same dispositions, and that gene pool will slowly come to dominate the lion population in that region.

None of this is "intentional": the lion has no conception of his own gene pool in competition with the pool represented by the cubs he found when he took over the pride. But that murderous behavior in fact, independently of all intention, favors his genes over those of other local lions. Then from an evolutionary perspective, killing the cubs is the *right* thing for the lion to do. (We know that all mammals are closely related on the evolutionary tree; does that mean that human stepfathers, and possibly stepmothers, whether or not they act on them, will have inclinations to abuse or get rid of their adopted children? Yes; our fairy tales are full of "wicked stepfathers" and "wicked stepmothers" who do just that.)

How can we tease out what of the behavioral dispositions of lions, or of ourselves, are the products of our evolution? The method by which such determinations are normally made and argued is the "thought experiment." Imagine two individuals in the "ancestral environment," that natural environment that prevailed during the period in which the species evolution actually took place (for humans, Robert Wright suggests, the environment was that of the small tribe, or clan, living as foragers, at some distance from other clans).[1] Imagine two lions, we begin. One

---

[1] The term, and its specification, are taken from Robert Wright, *The Moral Animal; Why We Are the Way We Are—The New Science of Evolutionary Psychology,* New York: Random House, 1994. This work is the general source for the rest of this section.

of them has no interest in mating with lionesses, the other has a lively interest in doing just that. Which one's genes will show up in the next generation? Then imagine two others, who have just taken over prides. One of them is a gentle and loving stepfather to all the cubs he finds in the pride, the other kills all those cubs and mates with the lionesses to sire his own. Which one's genes will predominate in the next generation?

But what of the lionesses? If it's all about preserving one's genes, i.e. preserving one's offspring, how do the lionesses take to the idea of having their cubs killed? Not very well; they try to prevent it. Interestingly, if most of the lionesses in the pride have small cubs at the time the pride is taken over, they may collectively oppose the lion, and delay the killing. Even more interestingly, if most of them don't have cubs, these will oppose the lionesses that do, so that the cub-killing may proceed and the lion can get them pregnant. (During the killing, the mother lionesses watch impassively; when it is over, they go to the bodies of their cubs, and eat them. Try that thought experiment: if there are two lionesses with dead cubs, and one buries her cubs and grieves for weeks while the other eats her cubs, which one will be in better physical shape to bear the next litter?) It works for humans, too. One person has the sense to come in out of the snow, the other doesn't. One mother takes conscientious care of her children, the other does not. We ask the same questions. (The game becomes more interesting when we get to survival of groups, below.)

Is human morality similarly evolved? This is a subject bursting with controversies; for our purposes here, we may ignore them and continue applying the same method.[2] Morality in its original understanding has to do with duties to others; the arrival of "duties to oneself" is late in the game. So to talk about morality is to talk about human groups, starting with the foraging clan wandering the savannahs and mountains of Africa, as presupposed by Wright. Does a willingness to sacrifice one's own interests for the welfare of the group have any evolutionary credentials? Start out with two humans (young men, we may assume), each of which is approached by a hungry bear. One of them departs the area quickly and climbs a tree, the other elects to wrestle with the bear. Clearly the genes of the tree-climber have a better chance of reaching the next generation. But now transfer the problem to the group and the village. Approached by a bear, or an enemy, if the young men will stand their ground and fight, the chances of keeping their genes **or what is the same thing, the genes of their families**, in the next generation are vastly improved. Even if the fight is against a much larger group of the enemy and therefore not to be won, the work of the warriors may delay the enemy long enough for the women and children, the actual bearers of the genes, to get to a place of safety. At least, the probabilities lean in that direction. We may add to this calculation the possibility that young men (and the young males of related primates) are by nature

---

[2] The classic work in the field is E. O. Wilson's *Sociobiology: The New Synthesis,* Cambridge, MA: Harvard University Press, 1975. The book aroused so much controversy that the term practically disappeared from the language in the years that followed.

quite irrationally brave at this age, unable, as long as they are in company with other young men of the village, to see any real danger to themselves. Can such irrational bravery also proceed from a genetic disposition? Yes.

Self-sacrifice for the preservation of the group has many precedents in pre-human nature; the earliest anthropologists noted the behavior of bees, where a designated group of guards or warriors will instantly attack any invader to the hive, even though a bee cannot sting without sacrificing her life. That tendency, to attack and sting regardless of the cost to the individual, is clearly innate (that's one of the advantages of drawing conclusions from work with insects, who simply do not have time in their short lives to learn anything), which means that the mechanisms for altruistic behavior exist in natural genomes, which means that there is no reason why they cannot exist in us.

The existence of a group linked closely by kinship also explains the origins of the most basic norms of morality. Within the bosom of the family, an ethic of avoiding harm and beneficence must prevail, or the family will go out of existence. (As we shall see, Aristotle identified the "Household," his original form of human association, as the group whose guiding ethic was the nurturing of every individual member.) No human being can live apart from all others; humans need social support just to survive, whatever the situation of physical resources might be. The ethic of self-sacrifice begins here, as all the family's resources are dedicated to the one most in need—the child with leukemia, or the start of a family enterprise. The fact that it is the group most closely linked by genetics that exemplifies the strongest ethic of mutual support explains—or is explained by—the evolved dedication to the preservation of the group's genes. Aristotle treated the Tribe, or tribal Village, as essentially an extension of the family, which in historical fact it usually is. The Village level adds levels of symbolic identification, including a narrative of origin, mission and destiny, to the extended family, increasing its hold on the loyalty and sacrifice of the individual members.

Robert Wright's major thesis in *The Moral Animal* is that at the point we feel most free and in control of our choices—in the choosing of sexual partners—we exemplify the power of inherited preferences based on the establishment of the future of the gene pool. Why do we choose the sexual partners that we do, and prefer the kinds of sexual activity that we prefer? The answers turn out to be very different for men and for women. In humans, the male is the aggressor, desiring and obtaining sexual intercourse with as many females as possible. The female is reserved, "coy," choosy about sexual partners. The male prefers partners who are younger, "beautiful," "sexy," "would be fun in bed." Female pornography sells well to men. The female prefers partners who are older, masters of their domains, rich and powerful. Male pornography does not sell to women, only to other men. Our cultural norms permit, indeed establish, a "double standard" for the sexes: men may seek multiple unions, while women must stick to one man alone. (A corollary of the double standard: a man who succeeds in having intercourse with many women is praiseworthy, a real man, while a woman who has intercourse with many men is a whore, despised by men and women both, unfit for any committed union.) A further corollary calls attention to an odd feature of cultural life, here or more especially in less developed nations: the more powerful the man—through wealth, office, or popular acclaim (think basketball players)—the more attractive he will be to women, so the more women he will accumulate, and (like that lion) will endeavor to make sure that other men do not have access to them. Hence the institution of polygamy in many societies; we remember that Osama bin Laden, chief perpetrator of the 09/11/01 attack on the World Trade Center in Manhattan, was the 17th child of his father, who had 22 wives. Where monogamy is the law, powerful men engage in serial polygamy, divorcing their wives as they age and marrying much younger, sexier, women.

These variant standards, condemned by anyone who has thought about them as hypocritical in the extreme, are easy to explain in the light of evolutionary drivers. Men's desires have evolved along with the rest of their genetic endowment, to favor as many sexual partners as possible: the more partners, the greater the possibility of offspring bearing their genes. In tandem, men's desires specifically exclude from any long-term union women who may be carrying offspring of other men ("whores"); human men are no more happy than male lions about raising other males' cubs. Women, on the other hand, can have only so many children, and each child requires an enormous investment of physical effort and resources to bring to maturity, a project that in most cases will require protection and the support of a male. Every child she bears will have her genes, so she has no need to expand the number of men in her bed. Further, she has discovered the male propensity to resent the sexual activity of other men where she is concerned, and will prudently refrain from activities which risk losing support and protection for the growing children.

Reasoning backwards from the choices that establish the parental genes in the next generation, more sexual choices become clear. What, after all, is a "sexy" woman? She is young, just entering onto reproductive age, she is healthy, indicated by a thousand attractive clues—complexion, hair, teeth, physical grace—she will be able to bear many healthy children. What about the powerful man, to whom the woman is attracted? He is older but very "fit," indicated by success in the world, he is strong and can repel other men, ensuring that the woman will not be forced into a union with another man who might destroy her offspring (remember that lion), his success will ensure continued support for her growing children, who will not be independent for the length of human childhood and adolescence, extraordinarily long by mammalian standards.

So sexual attraction, the psychological (dispositional) component of human sexuality, is as much evolved, determined by natural selection millions of years ago, as our opposable thumbs and lockable knees. We are what we have to be, and we want what we have to want, to ensure the best possible position on this earth for our own children, grandchildren, on to the seventh generation. Moral psychology may as well begin here, with inborn evolved tendencies which can lead to much virtue (in a life dedicated to supporting a spouse and lovingly raising children), and also much sin, both built into the human genome by the struggle for survival.

Why do we need to know this? Because before we start preaching the gospel of hope, faith, charity and the Belmont Principles, we need to know what we're up against. If we want people to be altruistic, we are going to have to set up the community mechanisms and institutions that will encourage and reward this virtue. If we want men to be monogamous, and forbear from attempting to have sex with every attractive woman they see, we have our work cut out for us. (As we are beginning to learn in our national life, the more powerful the man, the greater the temptations, and high visibility and universal condemnation will not prevent succumbing to them.) The next section will consider how we work toward the education of people who will practice virtue and abstain from vice.

4.2 Acquiring Morals: The Track of Education

How do we become moral people, adults who can be trusted with their own lives and the lives of other people? This is a question that has fascinated legions of scholars; we find a useful start toward an answer in a combination of the structures suggested by Aristotle (in the *Nicomachean Ethics* and the first book of the *Politics*), Lawrence Kohlberg, a 20th century psychologist, with contributions as appropriate from evolutionary biology, anthropology, and the reflections of contemporary moral psychologists and neurophysiologists.

The most primitive reactions we can find are taught. Even under the microscope of contemporary neuropsychology (of which more in the next section), focused on the portions of the brain that light up brainscans in response to certain sorts of stimulus, we find learned reactions. Consider that the amygdala, an almond-shaped set of neurons located deep in the brain's medial temporal lobe, part of the brain's limbic system (shown to play a key role in the processing of emotions, linked to fear and pleasure), "reliably responds to threatening visual stimuli such as snakes and faces of outgroup members."[3] We doubt that fear of snakes is genetic or inborn. But fear of an **outgroup,** recognizable by face, cannot possibly be inborn—how would the amygdala know what counts as an "outgroup" for any given person? So our primitive visual recognition of "bad" and "good" is learned, and at a very early age. The best explanation of such learning is that some emotions—fear is one of them—are communicated physically, non-verbally: the mother holding the child is frightened by something she sees, and that fear is instantaneously communicated to the child, who learns to react the same way.

---

[3] The passage is concerned with "alarm-bell emotions," emotional reactions that reject some object or action as morally unacceptable or disgusting (like eating feces); these emotions have been identified with "the amygdala, which has been implicated in responses to personal moral dilemmas, [and which] reliably responds to threatening visual stimuli such as snakes and faces of outgroup members." John Doris, ed., *The Moral Psychology Handbook,* Oxford, UK: Oxford University Press, 2012, p. 62; in Chap. 2, Fiery Cushman, Liane Young, and Joshua D. Greene, "Multi-System Moral Psychology." These authors in turn cite Le Doux, 1996 [Le Doux, J., *The Emotional Brain,* New York: Simon and Schuster, 1996] 166; and Phelps et al., 2000 [Phelps, E.A., O'Connor, K.J., Cunningham, W.A., Funayama, E.S., Gatenby, J.C., Gore, J.C., et al. "Performance on indirect measures of race evaluation predicts amygdala activation," *Journal of Cognitive Neuroscience,* 12(5):729–738 (2000)].

(That kind of learning may continue for some time; where members of the outgroup inhabit the same streets as the ingroup, adult ingroup members report mothers suddenly tightening the grip on the child's hand and pulling him away from an outgroup member, teaching fear and hatred by the gesture.) The emotion that accompanies that reaction is known to the moral psychologists as an "alarm-bell" emotion: it stops action in its tracks, and does not permit discussion.

Then racism (essentially) is one of the first things the child is taught? Yes, and the moral psychologist's favorite explanation accounts for it: our primitive reactions persist because during most of the human being's time on this earth, the 100,000 years preceding sedentism (settling in permanent communities), humans were as much prey as predators, and their worst enemies were those of their own species from competing groups. Survival advantage went to those groups who could recognize enemies quickly, and immediately arrange to fight or to make themselves scarce. By the laws of evolution, then, over the long run, the group that is acutely conscious of the distinction between those who are members and those who are not will persist into the future, and the group that is not will not. That conclusion, of course, is based on probabilities; but over the course of several millennia, probabilities work out.

We're just getting started on the subject of moral psychology, and already its conclusions cry out for ethical evaluation. Are we being told, not only that all humans "naturally" want to kill stepchildren, and that men are naturally unfaithful to wives who have been promised faithfulness, but also that our first lesson in morals is racism? Yes. Nowhere in the human genome is there an impulse to do justice, love mercy, and walk humbly with God, **except insofar as variations of these can be derived from evolutionary advantage**, which, we recall, has nothing to do with intentions or even consciousness. One of the aims of this chapter is to build the explanatory structures that will bridge the human nature we find and the human person we want to bring into being and help to flourish. In the meantime, we should shed any illusions we may have had that humans are "naturally" good, or innocent, and need only protection from evil influences to live good moral lives in complete freedom—a view that Jean-Jacques Rousseau might have espoused. The evident requirement for human society is that it encourage praiseworthy behavior and firmly discourage blameworthy behavior; philosophers have labored to define "praiseworthy," the moral psychologists are now teaching us where to look for the "blameworthy," and the rest of us are passionately trying to find out how to encourage the one and discourage the other.

We begin, as in the first sections, with Socrates. In the course of his trial for disbelief in the city's gods and corruption of the youth of the city, Socrates describes his "daimon," or divine voice, generally identified with his conscience, that opposes wrong action; he mentions it because it is significant to him that the daimon has not opposed his conduct in Athens or during his trial:

> In the past the prophetic voice to which I have become accustomed has always been my constant companion, opposing me even in quite trivial things if I was going to take the wrong course. Now something has happened to me [the death penalty] which might be thought and is commonly considered to be a supreme calamity; yet neither when I left

home this morning, nor when I was taking my place here in the court, nor at any point in any part of my speech, did the divine sign oppose me... What do I suppose to be the explanation? I will tell you. I suspect that this thing that has happened to me is a blessing, and we are quite mistaken in supposing death to be an evil. I have good grounds for thinking this, because my accustomed sign could not have failed to oppose me if what I was doing had not been sure to bring some good result (*Apology,* 40a–c, trans Hugh Tredennick).

We note the limitations on the daimon: (1) It issues commands only to Socrates, not to all the world; (2) its commands apply to single acts or courses of action only, not to rules or general ethical orientations; and (3) it only operates negatively; it opposes acts, it does not command them. In short, it operates like the "alarm bell" emotions of the moral psychologists—fundamental and non-negotiable. We may take this as the original moral learning, on which all others are built.

Aristotle carries on the explanation of moral learning. In the *Politics* he divides human associations into three stages—the Household, encompassing the nuclear family and whatever others live with them (grandmothers, servants, slaves and the like), the Village, an extended family with a long history, defined by the narrative of its history, origins, and the gods that created it (we would recognize it as a Tribe), and the Polis, or state, brought into being late in the development of civilization, defined by law and justice. The moral learning with which we are concerned at present happens in the Household, and Aristotle takes up its description in the *Nicomachean Ethics.* To raise a virtuous man (Aristotle had a great deal of respect for women, but had them operating under a different description of virtue), you must begin by making sure that he knows that he must do what he is told. (Already certain kinds of handicap can put a halt to the process.) Then translate commands into standing orders, from "don't do that!" to "Never do that!" (Do not, for instance, play with snakes, chase bears, or associate with members of the out-group—whatever that group might be to you.) Contemplation of actions so forbidden should set off the "alarm bell" emotion. With the most important prohibitions firmly in place, the next step in upbringing is negotiation—teaching the child that certain kinds of behavior will be reliably rewarded. With this step, the emergence of reactions called "currency emotions" by the moral psychologists, it becomes possible to establish patterns of productive behavior without worrying that the new possibilities will re-open the option of the strong taboos.

Psychologist Lawrence Kohlberg (1927–1987) modeled his "levels of moral development" on the stages of cognitive development in children expounded by Swiss psychologist Jean Piaget (1896–1980). Kohlberg hypothesized that "moral development" proceeded in three major stages from childhood to adulthood, each stage divided into two parts as moral development proceeded. The first major stage centered on the infant's and toddler's aversion to pain and desire for pleasure, resulting in a primitive sort of act-utilitarianism: whatever invites punishment is "wrong," (first part), whatever brings sweets and smiles is "right" (second part). These two stages combined Kohlberg called the "pre-conventional" stage. They map neatly on Aristotle's first stages, to the point where settled habits guide right behavior in the child. Note that the child is not asked to articulate or understand the prescriptions and prohibitions.

The extent to which the child exhibits moral (approved) behavior at this point depends upon the consistency of the environment's reward-punishment implementation; in an orderly universe, the same behavior is always demanded, rewards are invariant, and failure to perform appropriately is always punished. In this stage the rules become internalized and are followed automatically, as a matter of **habit**. At the end of this stage of development, **if it goes well,** the child has a firm grasp of "morality," the pattern of expected acts and omissions that matches the template set by the environment. If it does not go well—if the home environment is chaotic, if the expectations are absent, unclear or unpredictably changing—the child may emerge on the social stage of development simply amoral, considering every demand to be merely the current preference of the adult making the demand, and open to negotiation.

Only if good habits are well established would Aristotle invite the youngster to consider the reasons for the rules. (The provision of reasons prior to the successful formation of habits he took to be merely an invitation to argument: if the child is given to understand that this behavior is desirable **only because of** the reasons supplied, then as soon as the child can think up better reasons **not** to do what the rules require, or why the reasons do not apply in this case, he is, or should be, as he thinks, excused from the demand for that behavior.) Accepting the reasons, and continuing to act as the rules require, gives the youngster a method to expand the range of the rule. If our family provides food for the local Food Bank every week because it is the "compassionate" thing to do, then the next time he sees an instance of human need that invites a compassionate response, he will be willing to provide that response. Further, since he can now explain to himself why he does what he does, he can make these choices his own, voluntarily, when before understanding the reasons, he had to take the worth of this behavior on faith. He now has the foundation of a moral character. If this step fails, he will have no way to answer challenges to his ingrained behavior as his life continues.

It is important to Aristotle that the growing child has models of virtue to emulate. These are provided by the level of association that supersedes and incorporates the household—the tribe, or village (what we might call "the community.") The tribe is united around a narrative, a story of how they came to be, and why (usually a story of creator gods who remain with the tribe to protect it). These stories explain the rituals that are part of the life of the village, the demands that are placed on the member of the village to serve and protect it, and the ultimate destiny of the tribal group. Usually the creation stories include the designation of the land the tribe is to occupy, and often how the members are to make their living. The stories of heroes that populate the tribal history, which the child learns from his family and tribal group, give him moral models to follow, people to imitate. It is worth noting that the content of moral obligation changes in the transition from Household to Village: the only obligation within the Household is the nurturing and protection of all its members, while the Village may demand sacrifices from the individual as part of his membership.

Kohlberg's account of this transition is more attuned to the Western experience of childhood and education. In ancient Athens, all education beyond the immediate family was arranged privately between the child's father and a private tutor, who may or may not have other students in his classes. In Western Europe and America, children "go to school," with other children the same age, and these "peers" become the reference group for correct behavior. As the child becomes socialized into groups of peers and playmates, "right" and "wrong" take on new meanings: whatever the group approves is "right," and all the child wants is to be praised and accepted as a "good boy" or "good girl." The peer group (under some form of adult guidance) has simply taken the place of the immediate family. Kohlberg assumes that all the playmates come from similar families, with similar sets of rules internalized, obedience to which is now habitual. If this is not the case—if the members of the "peer group" come from very different family (Village) backgrounds—socialization will have some very difficult times, for which Kohlberg is in no position to account. We must remember that the adults of the household in which the child was born and raised to this point are not operating on their own, in isolation from the rest of the community. Until very recent times, households were always part of an extended family, clan or tribe, and the ancient laws of the tribe governed what the child was taught. Neither Kohlberg, nor Aristotle, nor our evolutionary history, posited a time when children of different tribes, communities, or races, would be thrown together when still very young, to attempt to negotiate with each other some way to go along with the group while retaining the rules and traditions that they were raised to revere. No society has figured out a good way to handle this situation.

As the developing intellect is gradually brought to bear on the child's activities, the child absorbs "the rules" of his or her present arrangements; these rules govern the actions of the group and each individual in it, and create conflict when the group does not want to go along with the rules. The child's first experience of moral dilemmas may arise at this point—to go along with the group, or insist on adherence to the rule, on following "law and order"? In this stage, the idea of questioning the worth of a rule does not occur to the child. This stage Kohlberg called the "conventional" stage. Until the chaotic mixture of traditions that characterize contemporary society, there was no reason to go beyond it.

As the child advances into adolescence and approaches adulthood, he begins to think for himself, or rather, to begin to apply the concepts underlying the rules he has been following to a much wider range of circumstances. Kohlberg notes the possibility at this point of advancing to theoretical positions in which the entire rule system of the society can be questioned. What makes those rules "right," after all? If the virtue of "justice" has been learned to apply to dealings within the group at the "conventional" stage, then it becomes possible to envision a "better" set of rules—rules governed by **greater** fairness to all members of the community and possibly beyond. If the value of "liberty" has become part of the spectrum of social values—which in Aristotle's time, it would not have—then we can envision a society improved by removal of "useless" restrictions, making everyone happier. Still committed to the group, the adolescent may propose that the group sit down and decide on a "constitution," a framework of rules to which they all agree. Kohlberg characterized this fifth stage of moral development as "social contract" (where the basis of the rules is the agreement of those who will be bound by them) or "utilitarianism" (where the basis is the greater harmony of the rules with happiness, fairness and individual freedom). For Aristotle, the achievement of the ability to incorporate moral concepts into the character of the person—from adherence to just rules and performance of just actions to becoming a person of justice—was the desirable end product of moral education.

Kohlberg asserts the existence of yet a higher stage, the sixth and final level of moral development, which he identifies with "justice." On his understanding, the individual will proceed through the phases, from infancy to adulthood, pretty much in the order given. Of course we may find people, including many adults, in fact making decisions purely on the basis of pleasure or pain to themselves (for instance); Kohlberg recognized this, but these instances he characterized as "regression" to infantile thinking. On the whole, he assumed, methods of decision-making will follow growth to intellectual and moral adulthood.

Many writers have found it difficult to make sense of this last stage, in contrast to the stage preceding it, but Kohlberg's theory was in so much trouble with his own field of developmental psychology by this point that the controversy here probably made little difference. Developmental psychologists were simply unable to find any evidence that people in fact move regularly from one of his decision processes to the next, while there is abundant evidence that most adults make decisions according to all six of Kohlberg's stages of moral development, depending on their circumstances. (If I am slowing my automobile in an area known to hide traffic police looking for speeders, or choosing my breakfast cereal according to my tastes this morning, I am staying in the "pre-conventional" stage of moral thinking, and quite appropriately so.)

Other social scientists also challenged Kohlberg's conclusions. Carol Gilligan, who had done extensive work with the moral orientations of women, found in her research that women did not "advance" from concern with agreement among the group to a "principled" stand that asserted rules and universal laws and encouraged individuals to stand against the group where it seemed to be violating principles. In several surveys based on the cases Kohlberg used, many women felt the greater importance of nurturing and protecting the group, in an ethic more devoted to "caring" for each other than to any "universal laws." (Aristotle recognized this orientation, but confined it to the Household.) The ethics of communally oriented societies, like the Chinese, also strongly disagreed with Kohlberg's conclusions, holding such individual adherence to self-chosen "principles" to be no more than an extension of infantile selfishness. Philosophers also may object to Kohlberg's stages, pointing out the puzzling inconsistencies within them. (For instance, if any group, or nation, has ever heartily agreed to adopt rules that are contrary to human happiness in the long run and just plain wrong—and history provides us with many examples of that happening—the conflation of "social contract" justification for rules and "utilitarian" justification must fail. The two schemes are logically independent, and can easily conflict.)

For Aristotle, the third and final stage of human association, the Polis, provided the opportunity for the completion of progress toward the complete human life, the life of **deliberation and choice**. The Polis is formed, in its founding theory, not by biology (like the Household) nor yet by the gods and tradition (like the Village), but by human decision. The assumption is that the several tribal Villages of a region find a common purpose—usually defense against some larger entity, bolstered by a desire for a permanent common marketplace—so they agree to form a larger association, a Polis or State, whose members (Citizens) are bound not by blood, religion, history or any real loyalty to each other, but only by the recognition that the association is best for all of them. Since they come from a variety of tribal hierarchies, and distrust one another too much to accept each other's hierarchies, they insist that all their members shall be treated as kings—that is, they shall be treated as equals. Since they come from a variety of religions and moral codes, and are unwilling to accept the moral code of any single tribe, they must make laws for themselves, and agree to be governed by those laws. They must select their laws on the basis of "the just and the useful," i.e. by utilitarian reckoning, taking into account the claims of all the groups. All laws apply equally to all (the condition called **isonomia**), without regard to the privileged positions held by some members in their own tribes. The citizen must therefore live by reasoning—deliberating the benefits and costs of each proposed law—and by free choice, agreeing to the law by which he will be bound. The necessity of living by deliberation and choice in the public sphere reflects back upon the individual life and teaches the Citizen to live this way in his private life; human flourishing is defined by this achievement.

4.3 Failing to Acquire Morals: What Can Go Wrong

The excuses we present for a variety of human ills and failings often appeal to the inappropriateness of evolution. We have back pain because those spinal columns evolved for quadripedal ambulation. Boys (at least) love games of running around and throwing stones because that's how we hunted, when we had to make our living hunting without guns. Carpal tunnels are vulnerable to repetitive motion stress because we did not, in our formative period, ever have to make our living with computers. Now we see that the same excuses apply to our social dysfunctions. We evolved in small clans in villages; we did not evolve in cities; the Athenian invention of the law-governed Polis was an adaptation to an urban reality that emerged only in historical time, when all human evolution had come to an end. No wonder cities seem to be ungovernable; we're only just learning how to deal with them. We did not evolve in pluralistic societies. We certainly always recognized that there were tribes other than our own, and our usual relationship to those others (the "outgroups") was one of unremitting hostility and contempt, often erupting in warfare. Friendship with members of the outgroups was highly suspect, cooperation discouraged, and marriage out of the question. If that sounds a lot like relationships between certain groups today, well, that's the way it was meant to be. The notion that all humans are equally worthy, that we ought to be good neighbors regardless of race, creed, or color, that we ought not only to tolerate differences but celebrate them—UN days in the fourth grade classroom, hands across the water, learn to appreciate each other as individuals—that idea is radically new, and likely to be unstable in times of stress and scarce resources. We have always known how to make war on the outgroups; making peace is difficult, we're not sure we know how to do it, and given our suspicions about the outgroups attitudes and behavior, we're not really sure that we should. Individuals can cross freely into the territory and company of another group, at least when there is no war—to trade, to visit, to reinforce whatever bonds of peace may have been forged. But the villages as a whole must retain separation and distinction, or risk annihilation and the loss of all traditional identity. (The threat of loss of identity is sufficiently severe to start a war by itself if such assimilation is threatened.)

We may draw some tentative political conclusions from all of the above. The first forms of human association, the ones extant in the ancestral period, are the family and the tribal village, strongly connected by history and by genes. These we may call "natural," as having been on the scene before we were in any position to modify our associations. The state, or polis, is not natural, in this sense. It came about by human decision, as creating the possibility of a better life for humans, more peaceful and more prosperous. Without the threat of catastrophic destruction from some combination of the neighboring tribes, states could afford to build cities, bridges, international ports, even machines whose only purpose was to explore the surface of Mars. But human nature is not abolished, or significantly altered, by these possibilities. Ultimately we will trust no organization larger than the tribe, and will fight to protect the tribe (manifest especially in its religious traditions) any time it seems seriously threatened by the state or any other trans-tribal organization. (What else can explain the pervasive right-wing fear of the black helicopters of the United Nations, descending upon us to disarm us and force us into collectives?)

We know that it is not impossible to modify human behavior to conform with current objectives and political orientations; we just need to calibrate state-enforced incentives to ensure the behavior that is needed. But if we want to modify the nature itself—the instant recognition of outgroups as hostile (and contemptible and not worthy of moral consideration), the desire of the male to make as many women as possible objects of his sexual activity—we are going to find these tasks very difficult indeed. That's why we have to know what we are up against when we make the attempt.

4.4 The Work of the Moral Psychologists: The Trolley Dilemma

The empirical discipline, or science, of Moral Psychology, seems to be an invention of the late 20th century, starting to come into its own only in the first decade of the 21st. It took on directly the question, how **in fact** do people make moral decisions—decisions on matters that affected the lives and interests of others? Until this time, there had been a general assumption in the field that some sort of cognition, "thinking," that had brought such decisions into being, and that if the decisions often seemed to be bad ones, we had to teach better thinking. Hence the centuries-long effort, condensed into Chap. 1 of this work, to teach better thinking, through the understanding of the logic of ethical systems. But what if these systems, or any others we might think of, had nothing at all to do with moral decision making? Empirical studies in this century[4] reached the disconcerting conclusion that faced with a moral quandary (the most famous of which will occupy the next section), most people reach their decisions immediately, without thought, intuitively. The primary role of "intuition," emotion, suggested that the **affective** (emotional, feeling-oriented) aspects of any situation were the most important in any decision. (Philosophers had suspected this from Plato onwards, but now we had proof.) Reason comes into play after the decision has been made, in the effort to justify the decision to others (or to oneself).[5] Then what triggers the emotional reaction? Neuroscientists cite the amygdala, above, and "mirror neurons" that "lead us to feel pain when we see others suffering."[6] As we saw above, these structures tend to be very selective, producing positive vibrations for altruism when we see members of the ingroup suffering, most likely vibrations of glee when we see members of the outgroup suffering. Neurons will not give us morality.

One way to do empirical research in moral psychology is by the thought experiment, suggested above as the most accessible way to determine the behavioral products of biological evolution. A group of subjects is assembled and, in one form or another, presented with a hypothetical situation. The subjects' reactions to that situation are documented, summed and expounded, and then the investigator is at liberty to explore the reasons for the results, either with the subjects or on his own. The dilemma most discussed in the moral psychology literature is the "Trolley Problem," first presented by Philippa Foot in 1967, and elaborated in its most familiar form by Judith Jarvis Thomson in the succeeding decades.[7]

---

[4] We will not review the empirical studies on this point, certainly not in any quantitative treatment, as beyond the primary scope of this work. They are all available in recent scientific literature; check out the sources in the Bibliography for this chapter.

[5] There is a particularly good source for this conclusion: Jonathan Haidt, "The emotional dog and its rational tail: A social intuitionist approach to moral judgment," *Psychological Review*, Vol 108(4), Oct 2001, 814–834.

[6] This statement is from Jonathan Sacks, chief rabbi of the United Hebrew congregations of the Commonwealth and a member of the House of Lords, in a NY Times Op-Ed, "The Moral Animal," Monday, December 24, 2012. The writer goes on to say, "We are hard-wired for empathy. We are moral animals."

[7] Philippa Foot, "The Problem of Abortion and the Doctrine of the Double Effect," *Virtues and Vices* (Oxford: Basil Blaxkwell, 1978; originally appeared in *Oxford Review,* #5, 1967. Judith Jarvis Thomson, "Killing, Letting Die, and the Trolley Problem," 59 *The Monist* 204–217 (1976); "The Trolley Problem," 94 *Yale Law Journal* 1395–1415 (1985).

The problem generally follows this plot: (*Originally*) you are the driver of a trolley that has lost its brakes. You see that ahead of you is a crew of five men working on the tracks, all of whom will surely be killed if the trolley hits them. You have time to switch the trolley to another track on which one man is working. Should you elect to hit the one rather than the five? (*In later presentations*) you are a switchman, controlling which track the trolley will take. You see the runaway trolley headed for the five-man crew; you see the one person on the side track to which you can switch the trolley, if you choose. Should you? (*In yet later presentations*) you are a spectator standing on a bridge beneath which the runaway trolley must pass. You can't switch the trolley, and the only way you can stop it is by dropping a very heavy weight in front of it. Beside you on the bridge is a very fat man. (You are a slim little thing, of no use as an obstacle.) That fat man, if toppled over the rail of the bridge, would stop the trolley, but of course he would be killed. Should you push him in front of the trolley?

One interesting result from the numerous studies that have used this problem to test normal human reactions to ethical dilemmas is that most people will agree that if the action required to sacrifice the one to save the five is merely throwing a switch in some control center, then it should surely be done. But if it involves actually seizing a person and throwing him over the bridge, then it should not be done, or at least, many fewer of the subjects think that it should be done. Now, why? In the setup of the problem, you must choose to sacrifice one to save five, either way, and there cannot be any moral distinction between them. Yet the subjects insist that there is a moral difference. What is it?

The subjects are not articulate on the case, but researchers speculate that the subjects are distinguishing between a case where the intention is to save five crew members, and the death of the one is merely a side effect (collateral damage?), and a case where you must actively do harm, even kill a man by pushing him in front of the trolley, in order to accomplish a good end, the saving of the five. In order to make sense of this distinction, some writers appeal to the "**Doctrine of Double Effect**," a philosophical monstrosity which holds that if an action aimed at a good result has the unfortunate consequence of accomplishing unintended harm at the same time, it may still be justified as long as the ill effect is really unintended.[8] This doctrine is apparently the result of speculations in moral theology (calculating the weight the action puts on the conscience of the agent, given that it is forbidden to cause harm), and does nothing but mischief in ethics, completely subverting the duties of prudence and foresight, and making nonsense of the concept of culpable negligence. Consider, after all, that no teenage driver *intends* to

---

[8] The Trolley Problem, and this speculation to explain it, have unfortunately become almost accepted in the field, and are mentioned in several articles in Doris, *The Moral Psychology Handbook*, op.cit., occasionally including diagrams of trolley tracks, showing where the crews are standing. See Gilbert Harman, Kelby Mason, & Walter Sinnott-Armstrong, "Moral Reasoning," p. 206ff, esp pp. 223–225; the DDE, as they call it, also shows up in Erica Roedder and Gilbert Harman, "Linguistics and Moral Theory," pp. 286–287, described there as a "non-obvious" moral rule. It certainly is that.

run down pedestrians in his praiseworthy efforts to get to work on time—it just happens, unless he takes care that it should not.

An alternative speculation to explain this experimental result is that subjects have a built-in, hard-wired, aversion to *doing harm*, i.e. a strong avoidance reaction to hurting anyone, so they find it morally repugnant to push a man to his death, while not finding it morally repugnant to throw a switch that results in the death of that man.[9] I find this speculation as dubious as the first; we have already become acquainted with a human being who has no problems at all doing harm to any individual in the outgroup—as a matter of fact participates enthusiastically in such harm. Let's take the thought experiment a little further: suppose you are a committed Nazi (or a violent Islamist, to bring us up to date), and the fat man beside you on the bridge is a corpulent Jew. Would you have any hesitation in throwing him off the bridge? Not necessarily.

I would doubt that the subjects are implicitly, or unconsciously, appealing to the Doctrine of Double Effect, or reacting in accordance with some primary obligation to "do no harm." It seems more likely that the two scenarios elicit very different mental portrayals of the act of sacrificing-one-to-save-five: In the first, we have only to deal with an inanimate switch, which we can do; in the second we have to assault a very heavy man, struggle with him (he may be tempted to assault back), and the whole episode of flesh on struggling flesh is highly disagreeable. Most soldiers, for instance, would rather kill the enemy with drones than with bayonets, although the death is just the same.

What is the role of Ethical Theory, covered in Chap. 1? The role is not initially extensive. For starters, *any* theory must accord with our moral intuitions, an assertion proved as far as it may be in William Gass's (1957) essay, "The Case of the Obliging Stranger." In this essay, Gass invites us to

imagine I approach a stranger on the street and say to him. "If you please sir, I desire to perform an experiment with your aid." The stranger is obliging, and I lead him away. In a dark place conveniently by, I strike his head with the broad of an axe and cart him home. I place him, buttered and trussed, in an ample electric oven. The thermostat reads 450 F. Thereupon I go off forget all about the obliging stranger in the stove. When I return, I realize that I have overbaked my specimen, and the experiment, alas, is ruined.
Something has been done wrong. Or something wrong has been done.
Any ethic that does not roundly condemn my action is vicious. It is interesting that none is vicious for this reason. It is also interesting that no more convincing refutation of any ethic could be given than by showing that it approved of my baking the obliging stranger.[10]

In the end, we are all intuitionists, at least in this basic sense. The major role of ethical theory is to provide a corrective to unbridled intuition, by insisting that any decision taken must be justified to the world in logical terms—"this is just how I feel" is not a justification, even if you feel that way very strongly indeed.

[9] Cushman, Young and Greene, op.cit. pp. 62, 63.
[10] William H. Gass, "The Case of the Obliging Stranger," *Philosophical Review* 66 (1957) 193–204.

4.5 Conclusion

Then how can we help people become more moral? Note that the task includes several impossibilities. One of my favorite daydreams is the re-establishment of tribal communities, in which children grow up following the rules of the tribal group and learn how to be noble self-sacrificing persons of firm character before they are ever required to participate in the larger multi-racial, multi-religious, world of UN Days. (And those who find such multi-ethnic and multi-ethic worlds disagreeable may elect to stay in that restricted community all their lives, assured that it will never be uprooted or forced to change; there would have to be physical boundaries to protect their land, like Indian reservations.) That's not going to happen. We live in a cosmopolitan world and we must adapt to it, and it does not seem that evolution is going to be any help on this point.

Another impossibility is a successful project to change human nature, by careful instructed child-rearing (inspired, possibly by monastic life?), reinforced with psychotherapy for those who find it impossible to stop thinking about the violent destruction of those who annoy them or future sexual conquests apart from marriage. This is not going to work either. Evolution has had millennia to imprint our nature, and no feeble efforts on our part now are going to change it. (Besides, we'd have to exterminate prior to sexual maturity all those who showed no progress toward the peaceful and self-controlled people we want, and that would be disagreeable.)[11]

On the other hand, we could certainly set up our education and laws to forbid the carrying out of anti-social fantasies, where the acts involved are harmful to the commonweal. Of course we already have laws against murder and mayhem, and they do not seem to be universally effective, even with the aid of psychotherapy. Further, there are limits on any measures we adopt. We have decided, for reasons that I know and respect, that protecting privacy and freedom of speech, even when the speech is hateful and borders on incitement to riot, is more important than rooting out the evil in men's minds. We have carefully limited our own ability to shape society and all the people in it according to our understanding of the best way for people to live, and given the extravagant errors made in the past by peoples with no such restraints, that is probably a good thing.

What can we do to help people better themselves and their world? The most effective education seems to be in stories. We have always told stories to children—as above, stories of the heroes who created or defended our people, stories of the dragons they slew and the helpless people (usually maidens) that they rescued, stories of their tireless labors to create a better world, all accompanied by stern injunctions to go and do likewise. Stories and plays, dramatic enactments of the kinds of virtues we want to inspire and preserve, and sympathetic portrayals

---

[11] But appropriate institutions have been imagined. See Sheri Tepper, *The Gate to Women's Country*, Victor Gollancz Ltd 2013 (1988).

of the members of the outgroup, whatever group that may presently be to us, are indeed effective in changing us.

One of the most surprising and gratifying qualities of the human animal is our continuing effort, noted by many of the philosophers, to become better, more moral, than we are. No other animal does this. It is a gift worth celebrating and a project worth encouraging.

Bibliography

Aquinas T Summa Theologica IA IIAE QQ 55–67; 90–96
Aristotle The nicomachean ethics; the politics
Edward Freeman R Stakeholder theory
Hobbes T Leviathan
Kant I (1785) Groundwork of the metaphysics of morals
Locke J Second treatise (of civil government)
Mill JS (1863) Utilitarianism; on liberty
Rawls J (1970) A theory of justice
Ross WD The right and the good

L. Newton, *Ethical Decision Making: Introduction to Cases and Concepts in Ethics*,
SpringerBriefs in Ethics, DOI: 10.1007/978-3-319-00167-8, © The Author(s) 2013

Printed by Printforce, the Netherlands